BALDUR'S LAST VOYAGE.

THE NINE WORLDS

STORIES FROM NORSE MYTHOLOGY

BY

MARY E. LITCHFIELD

Fredonia Books
Amsterdam, The Netherlands

The Nine Worlds
Stories From Norse Mythology

by
Mary E. Litchfield

ISBN 1-58963-148-X

Reprinted from the 1890 edition

Fredonia Books
Amsterdam, The Netherlands
http://www.fredoniabooks.com

In order to make original editions of historical works
available to scholars at an economical price, this
facsimile of the original edition of 1890 is
reproduced from the best available copy and has
been digitally enhanced to improve legibility, but the
text remains unaltered to retain historical
authenticity.

" I THINK Scandinavian paganism, to us here, is more interesting
than any other. It is, for one thing, the latest. It continued in
these regions of Europe till the eleventh century: eight hundred
years ago the Norwegians were still worshippers of Odin. It is
interesting also as the creed of our fathers, the men whose blood
still runs in our veins, whom doubtless we still resemble in so many
ways. . . .

" Neither is-there no use in *knowing* something about this old
paganism of our fathers. Unconsciously, and combined with higher
things, it is in *us* yet, that old faith withal. To know it consciously
brings us into closer and clearer relations with the past, — with our
own possessions in the past. . . ." — THOMAS CARLYLE.

iv

PREFACE.

In writing these stories of the Norse gods, many books have been consulted, and especially the following : Anderson's Norse Mythology, the translation of Rydberg's Teutonic Mythology and of the Younger Edda by the same author, Grimm's Teutonic Mythology, translated by Stallybrass, and Thorpe's translation of Sæmund's Edda.

My aim has been to write a story simple enough for children, but not so simple as to be uninteresting to older persons. My own interest in Norse mythology was aroused many years ago by two books, "Heroes of Asgard" by A. and E. Keary and "Wonderful Stories of Northern Lands" by Julia Goddard. The excuse for this book is, that, in many respects, it is unlike any that have been written on the same subject. And this is partly owing to the fact that Rydberg's researches have made it possible, for the first time, for one to form a definite conception of the cosmography of the mythology, and also because he clears away many inconsistencies that have long clung to it.

I have written the story of the gods as it has formed itself in my mind after much reading and thinking. In some cases the words of the poems of Sæmund's Edda have been used, especially in the last chapter, The Twilight of the Gods. I have taken the liberty of putting a part of the " Vala's Proph-

ecy " and of other prophecies into the mouth of Odin, because
he is represented in the Eddas as knowing all that is to come
in the future. In the story of Baldur, I have followed Rydberg
rather than the author of the Younger Edda. Rydberg claims
that the latter has departed from the old mythology in many
instances, and especially in his version of the Baldur myth.
In order to make a dramatic whole out of the separate stories,
it has been necessary to supply connecting links and to give
special prominence to certain characters. Loki is the central
figure ; and Thiassi, as portrayed by Rydberg, plays an important part. Whatever is coarse or unpoetic in the old stories
has been left out, and much has been added from my own
imagination. For instance, there is no foundation for the
chapter, Odin seeks Wisdom from Mimir, except in the lines
quoted from Odin's Rune-song.

I wish to express my sincere thanks to those who have kindly
answered my questions, or helped me by their criticisms.

CONTENTS.

THE NINE WORLDS.

STORIES FROM NORSE MYTHOLOGY.

INTRODUCTORY CHAPTER.

OUR ancestors who lived hundreds of years ago believed in many gods. The stories of these gods, however, were written, not in sacred books, but in the memories of the people ; for in those early days the Teutons living in northern Europe had no written lan-guage.[1] For centuries the fathers handed down to their children the traditions they had received from former generations ; until finally. Christianity took the place of the old religion.

Even after this, the belief in the gods lingered long in out-of-the-way places ; and, at last, in Iceland, some of the stories about them were collected and written down. The books in which they are written are called Eddas. There are two of them, — The Elder, or Sæmund's Edda, which consists of poems, and The Younger, or Snorre Sturleson's Edda, which is prose.

---

[1] They had a few characters called *runes,* that were supposed to possess magic properties.

Probably these stories collected in Iceland are not just like those told hundreds of years before in Europe, because things handed down by word of mouth are sure to change a little with each generation.   Still, they give us, in the main, a true idea of the gods our warlike forefathers believed in.   The stories that follow in this book are for the most part based upon the Eddas.

Our ancestors knew but little of the world, and what they saw made them think that it was flat, — a great flat region encircled by a river, called the Ocean. They believed that there were nine worlds instead of one, arranged in some such way as this:[1] —

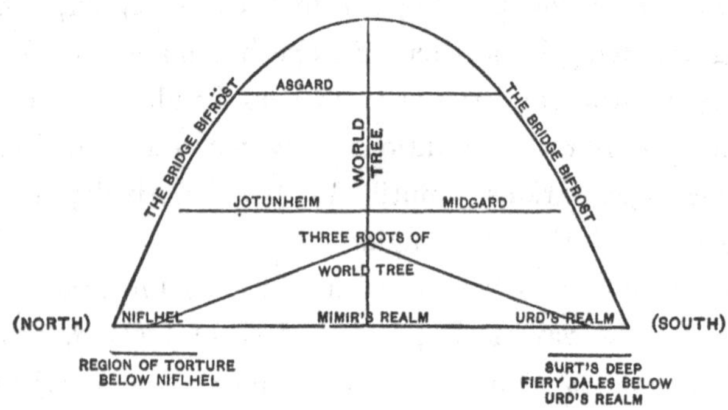

Highest of all was Asgard, the home of the Æsir, or gods, ruled over by Odin, or Wodan.

Next below came Midgard, the world of men, with the river, Ocean, around it.   Beyond the Ocean, on the same plane, was Jötunheim, the upper giant-world.

---

[1] In the plan of the nine worlds Rydberg has been followed.

Far below these, stretched the under-world, vast compared with the regions above it, and containing four of the nine worlds.   In the north was Niflheim, the

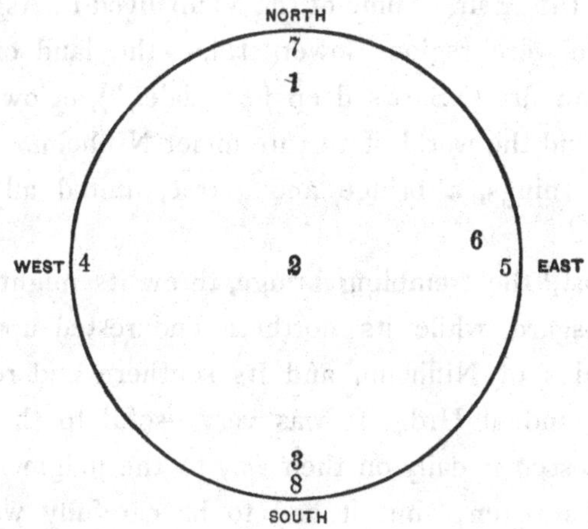

(1) Spring Hvergelmir, in Niflhel or Niflheim, under Yggdrasil's northern root.
(2) Well of Wisdom in Mimir's Realm, under Yggdrasil's middle root.
(3) Urd's Well in her Realm, under Yggdrasil's southern root.
(4) Home of the Vanir.
(5) Home of the Elves in Mimir's Realm.
(6) Castle where Baldur dwelt with the Asmégir.
(7) Northern End of Bifrost, guarded by Heimdall.
(8) Southern End of Bifrost, near Urd's Well.

lower giant-world, cold, dark, and misty. In the south Urd and her two sisters ruled over the kingdoms of the dead. Between these two regions lay Mimir's land, where, besides the wise old giant, there dwelt many mighty beings, among whom were Night (the ancient mother), bright Day, and Delling, the elf of the dawn.

Even the Sun and Moon had resting-places there ; and in some parts there were elves and dwarfs. West of Mimir's land was the home of the Vanir, a noble race akin to the Æsir. Some of the Vanir lived in Asgard.

There were regions lower still, — the land of sub-terranean fire ("Surt's deep fiery dales"), below Urd's realm, and the world of torture under Niflheim.

Two things, a bridge and a tree, united all these worlds.

Bifröst,[1] the trembling bridge, threw its mighty arch over Asgard, while its northern end rested upon the mountains of Niflheim, and its southern end reached to the land of Urd. It was very useful to the gods, who crossed it daily on their way to the judgment hall in Urd's realm; but it had to be carefully watched lest hostile giants should, by its help, find their way to Asgard. Heimdall, a pure and wise Van, guarded its northern end. His ears were so good that he could hear the grass pushing up through the ground, and the wool growing on the backs of the sheep; and he needed less sleep than a bird.

The tree which connected the nine worlds was called Yggdrasil.[2] Its three main roots were watered by three fountains in the under-world, and the rootlets went

---

[1] Rydberg maintains that the Milky Way, and not the rainbow, is the original of Bifröst.

[2] Yggdrasil was an ash-tree.

down to Surt's deep dales and to the world of torture. The branches of this wonderful tree reached
to the most remote regions, and its sap carried life
everywhere. Serpents gnawed its roots; stags, squir-
rels, and birds lived among its branches; and on its
topmost bough, far above Asgard, the cock Vidofnir
glittered. It was indeed a "tree of life."

They had a strange story of the creation, these
northern people, — a story that is interesting because
it is so very old.

In the beginning there were two worlds, — a world of
freezing mists in the north, and a world of raging fire
in the south. Between these two regions was a yawning abyss, — Ginungagap, dark and empty.

In Niflheim, the cold world, a mighty spring sent
down twelve rivers; and some of the rivers flowed into
the abyss, filling the part that was next Niflheim with
layers of frozen vapor. The flames raged so fiercely in
Muspelheim, the world of fire, that they blew over into
Ginungagap, taking many sparks with them. At last
the sparks met the frozen vapor, and a huge giant was
formed. His name was Ymir.

The following lines are from a translation of one of
the old poems : —

> There was in times of old
> where Ymir dwelt
> nor sand nor sea

> nor gelid waves;
> earth existed not,
> nor heaven above,
> 'twas a chaotic chasm
> before Bur's sons
> raised up heaven's vault,
> they who the noble
> mid-earth shaped.[1]

Not long after the creation of Ymir, a cow, Aud-humla, was formed; and the giant Ymir fed upon her milk. The cow licked the masses of frozen vapor, for they were salt. And as she was licking, the first evening, a man's hair appeared; and the second day his head; and the third day the whole man could be seen. His name was Bur. He was very large and fair and had great strength. He had a son called Bor.

From under the arm of the huge giant Ymir there grew two children, a boy and a girl. They were giants, but still they were good, and from them descended many wonderful beings. Mimir, the boy, grew to be the wisest person in all the nine worlds. Unfortunately he lost his life in a great war. Odin cut off his head and preserved it; and it kept on giving good advice, as though it were Mimir himself. The great goddess Night was Mimir's daughter. The girl who came from

---

[1] From the Völuspâ in Thorpe's translation of Sæmund's Edda.

under Ymir's arm was called Bestla. She was the mother of Odin.

While a race of good and wise giants descended from Mimir and Bestla, a race of evil giants and monsters came from a six-headed son of Ymir's. This monster grew from Ymir's feet. His descendants were so powerful that in the end they were to conquer Odin and cause the destruction of the world. The ruin of the gods, however, was to be brought about in part by their own shortcomings: they were not strong and noble enough to resist the evil forces arrayed against them.

Odin and his two brothers slew the giant Ymir, dragged his body into the middle of the abyss, and from it formed the world.

> From Ymir's flesh
> the earth was formed,
> and from his bones the hills,
> the heaven from the skull
> of that ice-cold giant,
> and from his blood the sea.[1]

The "melancholy clouds" were formed from Ymir's brains. Some of the sparks that flew over into Ginungagap were placed in the heavens, and men called them stars.

[1] From The Lay of Vafthrûdnir in Thorpe's translation of Sæmund's Edda.

One day Odin and his brothers[1] were walking near the sea, when they came upon two trees, an ash and an elm. From these trees they created the first human beings, — a man and a woman. An old poem says : —

> They found on earth,
> nearly powerless,
> Ask and Embla,
> void of destiny.
> Spirit they possessed not,
> sense they had not,
> blood nor motive powers,
> nor goodly color.
> Spirit gave Odin,
> sense gave Hœnir,
> blood gave Lodur
> and goodly color.[2]

The elves and dwarfs swarmed in Ymir's body after he was killed : they were not created by the gods.

In Europe there are still ancient customs and old sayings that go back to the time when men believed in Thor and Odin. In some parts of Germany, until recently, the peasants left a clump of grain standing for Odin's horse when they gathered the harvest. Even here in America there is something to remind us of the old gods. Tuesday is named for Tyr, the god

[1] Rydberg maintains that Hœnir and Lodur are identical with Vili and Ve, Odin's brothers.

[2] From the Völuspá in Thorpe's translation of Sæmund's Edda.

who gave his right hand to save his people from the dangerous wolf. Wednesday is Odin's, or Wodan's, day. He placed wisdom above everything else, being willing to give even his eye for one drink from Mimir's well. Thursday belongs to Thor, the fierce thunder-god; and Friday to Frigga, Frey, or Freyia, — we are not sure which.

How did people come to believe in all these gods? No one will ever know just how the belief began and how it grew, but it is possible to learn something about it.

We who live now have had so many things found out for us, that we cannot imagine how the world seemed to people who knew very little, and who had to find out everything for themselves or make their own guesses about things. In the early ages men lived in a world of mystery; the sun, the moon, the sea, the wind, — everything was strange and wonderful. Life was a struggle. In the north it was hard to provide for the needs of the long, cold winter. Man had not learned how to control the forces of nature, and he was contin- ually warring against them. The mountains shut him in; the forests were dark and awful; the snow and the ice and the desolate wastes set themselves against him to thwart his best endeavors. Was it strange that these hostile forces seemed like cold, heartless giants opposed to all that was joyous and gentle and human?

Thus began the belief in frost giants and mountain giants.

There were kindly powers, however, and chief among these was the sun, man's best friend. He gave man light and heat. Through his influence the rivers burst their bonds, the grass grew green, and the crops ripened. While the sun reigned, life was happy. But in the north, at a certain time of the year, the sun lost his power; and in the extreme north, he sank out of sight and left the world in darkness. As men saw him disappearing, what anxiety must have filled their hearts! How could they be sure that this mysterious being, upon whom their very lives depended, would ever return? How eagerly they must have watched for him; and when the first faint flush appeared, what rejoicing! No wonder they hailed the returning sun as a god, — the god who gave light and joy.

The character of Odin is said to have come from men's feeling about the sun. Some books say that Odin gave one of his eyes for the drink from Mimir's well, and that the sun represents Odin's single eye. We can easily see that the story of Iduna has something to do with the going and coming again of the summer.

Baldur is the god who represents most fully the feeling that men had for the sun in the far north. Baldur was the pure and shining god. And as the sun sank out of sight and left the world in darkness, so he died, and went to the under-world, causing untold grief in Asgard and Midgard.

The thunder was pictured as a strong, fierce god, with fiery hair and beard, who rode in his iron chariot, and flung his mighty hammer at the rocks and mountains, — Thor, the foe of the giants.

All the gods cannot be easily traced back to something in nature; indeed, most of them lost their original character as the years rolled on, and became very human in their attributes; and we must not think of them as representing to their worshippers simply some object in nature. Men and women lived hard lives in those rude times, and thought much about life, and death, and the unknown future. What they believed and hoped was expressed in the character of their gods, and in the pictures they made for themselves of the unseen worlds. As we read their poems and stories, we feel that they were trying to get at the secret of life, the great open secret that no one has wholly guessed, even with the "Light" that has come into the world since those days.

It was a fighting age. The hero looked forward to death on the battle-field as the greatest of blessings. He believed that so dying the Valkyries would come and take him to Odin's palace of Valhalla, where the fighting and the feasting would go on for ages. Still, with all their love of war, these people did not believe that force was to be victorious, or that evil was to triumph over good. The strong gods were to have their day, but were to be defeated at Ragnarok ; then Baldur was to come — the ruler of a new and better world. Goodness and purity were to conquer in the end.

All this has passed away, and those warlike people have left little to remind us that they once lived here. Yet one heritage we have, — not a few pyramids of stone, but nine worlds built of that airy stuff that outlasts solid granite, and peopled with beings strange and wonderful. Surely, he who loves the past will care sometimes to wander amid the shadows of those ancient worlds.

ODIN.

ODIN SEEKS WISDOM FROM MIMIR.

IT was night in Asgard, the home of the gods. A soft light fell upon the sleeping city, showing its vine-clad hills and glittering palaces, and touching even the deep, still valleys that lay between. For the trembling bridge, Bifröst, spanned the city like a rainbow of silver, meeting the horizon at the north and south. Toward the south, as far as the eye could reach, rose mountains, with castles upon their tops and sides; while, toward the north, stretched the level and grassy plains of Ida.

From a structure upon the highest place of the city, a shaft shot up, slender and glittering, as a tall spire rises from some great cathedral. It rose high above all the castles and towers, so high as almost to touch the arch of the celestial bridge. This slender shaft was Odin's High Seat. From its top could be seen not only Asgard, but also a large part of the worlds below.

Here the Allfather sat alone, buried in thought. Alone except for two wolves that lay sleeping at his feet, and two ravens [1] perched upon his shoulders, weary after their journey through the nine worlds.

[1] Odin's ravens were, Hugin (thought) and Munin (memory); each day they flew over the nine worlds, bringing back tidings to Odin.

After sitting a long while in meditation, Odin looked down upon the stately homes of his children, and upon the fields that stretched away, beyond the high walls and the dark, rushing river that surrounded the city of the gods. Then his eyes tried in vain to pierce the dense blackness that shrouded a land far below him toward the north. He gazed long and earnestly, and at last rose up and descended quickly to the palace just below his High Seat. The vast halls resounded as he strode through them.

He hastened to a building near by, and soon appeared again, leading a gray horse. This horse was well fitted to bear the father of the gods; for he had a powerful frame and eight legs. As he stood waiting for Odin to mount, he trembled with eagerness, and flames poured from his nostrils. In an instant Odin was on his back, and the wonderful horse was carrying him toward the north with the speed of the wind.

The high wall and the dark-river surrounding the city were no obstacle to Sleipnir. He leaped easily over them, and kept on his swift way across the fields on the other side, which stretched green and level to the distant horizon. Here and there were groves in whose quiet depths a less rapid traveller might have heard the trickling of fountains. And occasionally a lake reflected on its dark surface the silvery arch of Bifröst.

At last they reached the point where the celestial

bridge touched the outer edge of Asgard. The eight-footed horse rushed unhesitatingly upon the bridge, although it trembled beneath his weight, sending up fitful flames. Like a comet among the stars, Sleipnir sped on, bearing Odin over the black depths.

At length a faint light reached them from the north; and soon Odin saw a horseman, clad in a white garment, coming towards him. The horse had a mane of gold, which, shining full upon the rider, revealed his pure, pale face. Approaching, he said, "Welcome, Father Odin. I have been watching for you ever since I heard Sleipnir's eight hoofs strike the bridge. Doubtless some deep purpose brings you across Bifröst at night?"

"Yes, Heimdall, you have judged rightly," said Odin; "a great matter urges me on; and many days must I journey ere I return home. I must go through the dark land of our enemies, the frost giants of the lower world; and then far beyond, to regions that few have visited. Fortunate are the gods that Heimdall guards for them the trembling bridge. Were it not for your keen ears that hear the grass growing, and the wool thickening on the backs of the sheep, our enemies might, ere this, have crossed the abyss, and have stormed Asgard."

As he spoke, they both looked down upon the land beneath them, dark, except for the light that streamed from Heimdall's far-shining castle at the bridge-head.

And they could see the glistening tops of ice mountains rising above the mists.

As Odin looked he said, "Our enemies are strong, and I fear the treacherous Loki, who is ever going between Asgard and the giant-world. We have need of all your watchfulness, Heimdall, and of all the strength of Thor, the dread foe of the giants, to keep our enemies at bay. What great wisdom do I need to protect the realm of Asgard, and the world of men!"

They kept on their way toward Heimdall's castle, which was on a high mountain near the bridge-head. The castle was apparently made of the same material as the bridge, and, as it rose toward the sky, might have been taken for a structure of cloud bathed in moon-light. But in truth it shone with a soft fire of its own; for radiance streamed from it in all directions, lighting up, as we have seen, a part of the cold, foggy land of the giants. The approach to the bridge was in this way made so clearly visible that it would have been impossible for any one to get near without Heimdall's knowledge, even had his hearing been less keen. Then, too, the castle was strongly fortified, surrounded by a high wall, and a moat, the waters of which, like those of the Asgard river, were covered with a mist that flashed into flames when disturbed by an enemy of the gods.

"Come in, Odin," said Heimdall, as they reached the

castle; "your journey has been long, and a hard road lies before you."

They entered a large hall whose walls were made of something that resembled white marble or alabaster. All the decorations were of silver. Vines bearing clusters of silver grapes ran along the walls, and curious horns and lamps hung from the arches above. Tall youths, clad, like Heimdall, all in white, brought in tankards of foaming mead.[1]

The two gods drank the mead, and talked earnestly together, until at last Odin rose, saying, "One favor I ask of you, Heimdall: keep Sleipnir for me until my return. There are few to whom I would intrust him, but he will be safe with you. I wish to journey, unknown, through the world of cold and darkness, and the horse would betray me."

Heimdall accompanied Odin a short distance down the steep mountain, and then returned to his post, to guard the bridge of the gods.

As Odin went down into Niflheim,[2] a chilly fog closed about him, shutting out the light from Heimdall's castle, and making it hard for him to keep to the path. As he got lower, the cold became intense, and his foot slipped on the icy road which broadened into a river of ice. There were sounds of creaking and crashing, and

[1] Honey and water, fermented and flavored.
[2] The giant-world in the northern part of the great under-world.

in the distance could be heard the moaning of waves as they broke upon the desolate shore. As he made his way he could just distinguish through the mist and darkness the enormous mountains of ice surrounding him. Some of these seeming ice mountains were really frost giants whose huge heads would slowly turn to follow him. Once an iceberg in the sea went to pieces with the noise of distant thunder, and he could long hear the booming and crashing, Sometimes a deluge of icy water would rush upon him from a cascade that he had not perceived; and then he would hear the slow, heavy laughter of the giants, sounding like the roar of hoarse winds. At one point in his journey he came upon a field of ice; and as the fog lifted, he could see that it stretched on all sides, level and white, covered with snow. Here the sounds of creaking and crashing ceased, and he no longer heard the laughter of the giants: the silence was absolute. He stood alone under the stars.

After a long journey through the ice region, Odin reached a country where dark, savage mountains took the place of icebergs, and here and there on their peaks loomed up the strongholds of the mountain giants. As he kept on his way, he could sometimes distinguish the giants themselves, looking like huge, moving masses of rock. This land was as dreary as the land of ice; for although there was no fog, and a faint twilight glimmered, it was very desolate.   Not a green thing was to be seen; nothing but grim mountains and dark abysses, at the bottom of which rushed rivers, finding their way from the spring Hvergelmir to the cold northern sea. The mountains, at times, gave place to level wastes of great extent, where bowlders lay heaped one upon another, with deep, still pools lurking among them. Often heavy clouds rolled across the sky, enveloping the mountains.

After journeying long, Odin stood upon a high place from which he could look down upon a morass stretching as far as the eye could reach. In the dim light he could just distinguish a narrow footpath of solid ground leading across it.   When he was partly over, one of the giants saw him ; and soon a troop of the monsters came stumbling after him. Finding it impossible to reach him, they filled the air with their shouts, and brandished their great clubs. Upon this a fearful wind arose, threatening to blow Odin from the narrow path. Clouds shaped like dragons blew gusts at him from their open mouths ; and when he got safely over, howls of disappointed rage resounded long in the air behind.

He came next to a river, whose dark, swift current bore with it sharp stones and bits of iron, and no bridge spanned the deadly stream;   but Odin crossed it safely on some driftwood.

Higher mountains than any he had yet seen now

loomed up toward the south; and one, higher than the others, down whose sides rushed twelve rivers. On the top of this mountain was the ice-cold spring Hvergel-mir. One of the three roots of the great World Tree, Yggdrasil, was bathed by the waters of this spring; and the rivers that flowed from it went in all directions; some flowing through the cold, foggy land of the giants to the northern ocean, while others flowed toward the south, through the vast realms where Mimir [1] and Urd [2] guarded their wells under the other two roots of the World Tree.

As Odin neared the mountain, his way led through a gloomy cave, where he could hear the baying of a dog and the creaking of an iron gate. This gate, he knew, barred the descent to the world of torture below Nifl-heim, — a world far more dark and dreadful than that through which he had just passed. Once out of the cave, the road led over the mountain. On the highest peak stood a solitary watchman, the trusty guardian of the spring and the dread foe of the giants.

As Odin came near, he greeted him: "Did the mon-sters try to harm you, Odin? The hateful crew would be glad enough to crush the father of the gods and get possession of Asgard. And your Loki is too much

[1] The giant who grew from under Ymir's arm.

[2] Urd and her two sisters were norns, or fates, representing the past, present, and future.

with them.   I often see him there.   He thinks himself
well hidden by the darkness; but my eyes are trained
to see in the dark."

"Yes, Egil," replied Odin; "your eyes and Heimdall's ears are the best defence we have against our
foes. I came through safely, as you see. Their attacks
would have been more fierce had they known me. As
for Loki, I am well aware how dangerous he has become. Still, I may not yet turn him out of Asgard, for
I am bound by an oath made when we both were
young, — when I thought him innocent. But I must
hasten, Egil; a great purpose urges me on."

As Odin went down the southern slope of the mountain, a pleasant prospect greeted his eyes, wearied with
the gloomy sights upon which they had been looking
for so many days. The country was still mountainous,
but it was not black and sterile. Rich metals seamed
the rocks, and here and there were the mouths of
caves where sparkled crystals and gems. When Odin
stopped and listened, he could hear the picks and ham-
mers of the dwarfs. Twilight still hung over the scene,
but at intervals lights streamed across the sky, their
rich colors playing upon the mountains.

Odin had now to cross a broad river, and then he
could see in the distance a castle of fantastic shape,
which was ornamented in an unusual manner. Stone
dragons grinned from its corners, their large jewelled

eyes gleaming like fire as the lights flashed upon them. About the slender columns twined golden snakes and lizards of copper; and metal vines ran thickly along the walls, bearing gems for flowers. A fire shone from one part of the building, and it was evident that work of some kind was going on.

This strange castle was the home of Sindri and his brothers, — dwarfs, and famous artists, who had made wonderful weapons and ornaments for the gods. None approached them in skill except the sons of Ivaldi. The latter were partly of giant blood, and were said to be magicians as well as artists. Between them and the dwarfs there was some rivalry, but, as yet, no hard feeling. Odin passed near the castle, but did not enter.

As he went on, the mountains lost all their savage wildness, and rose in gentle outlines against the sky. They were clothed with forests and vineyards. Down their slopes rushed brooks, changing into cascades of mist. Peaceful valleys stretched between the mountains; while high above all were clouds, glowing with the colors of an eternal sunset. For this was a land where dark night and glaring midday never came.

The mountains gradually softened into hills, and these, at last, were lost in broad stretches of level fields covered with golden grain or tall, waving grass. The rivers glided along, deep and peaceful. Flowers bloomed everywhere, their bright colors reflected in the still waters of little ponds. Herds of deer came timidly up to Odin, and birds sang to him as he passed. Only the gentlest breeze stirred the leaves, and all sounds were low and sweet.

Along the southern horizon there now appeared a bank of white clouds, piled high, one upon another. But as Odin neared them, they changed to mountains of marble, evidently enclosing some sacred spot. Like pure white sentinels they stood, bathed with rich colors.

There seemed to be no entrance through this marble wall; but when Odin reached it, he knocked with his staff, and a door was opened. A man of grave and reverend aspect greeted him, and led the way through a spacious cave sparkling with crystals that reflected the light of his torch. At the further end of the cave was a door, larger than the one by which Odin had entered, opening into a circular valley.

The sides of the valley were formed by the marble mountains; but they did not look like mountains on the inside; for they had been carved into beautiful shapes, and delicate vines ran over them, veiling the whiteness of the marble.

From the centre of the valley grew the root of the enormous World Tree; and the waters of the deep well of wisdom bathed the root of the tree. At the further end of the valley rose a stately palace. Here and there were groups of trees, and rare plants bloomed on all sides. Near a pool a large turtle, his back covered with the incrustations of ages, basked lazily in the light. Harmless serpents with brilliant eyes twined about the trunks of trees. Dragons slept with folded wings, while many ancient and uncouth monsters rested amid the groves, or sunned themselves in the niches of the marble walls. Gay-colored birds flitted in and out among the branches, and peacocks walked proudly about, spreading their tails. The scene was made more fair by the light that fell upon it. It was not sunlight, and one could not tell whence it came; but it flooded the peaceful valley with the softest radiance.

Odin stood for a few moments looking at the scene before him, and then walked slowly toward the centre of the valley. Under the root of the World Tree sat a man of giant stature, apparently absorbed in watching the waters of the well. Long silver locks floated over his shoulders, and a white beard fell upon his breast. There was no look of old age in his face, although, as he raised his head, the wisdom of the centuries gleamed from his deep blue eyes, and his whole aspect expressed perfect peace. His hand rested upon the edge of the well, which was thickly overlaid with gold. Near him stood an immense chest, curiously carved, containing treasures from bygone ages. A large horn of silver lay upon the chest, bearing Heimdall's name in runic characters of gold.

As Odin came near, Mimir rose, saying, "Welcome, Odin! You come from the north, I see. This time you have chosen the hard road, and on foot too!"

"Yes, Mimir," answered Odin; "I chose that road because I wished to explore the land of my enemies, and I have come to you for counsel and help."

"Gladly will I help you, as you know," said Mimir.

"I know your readiness," replied Odin; "but this time I ask what no one has ever asked of you. My realm is beset with dangers. Loki grows in wickedness. He has taken for his wife the witch[1] of the Iron-wood, and their children threaten to prove our most formidable foes. And the frost giants and the mountain giants, as you know, are only too ready to attack us whenever there is a chance of success. I need great wisdom rightly to govern and protect Asgard, and Midgard, the world of men."

Both were silent for a moment; and then Odin said, looking earnestly at Mimir, "In order that I may gain this wisdom, I ask for one drink from your deep well."

After a long silence, Mimir said slowly, "You have asked a great thing, Odin! Are you prepared to pay the price for it?"

[1] The principle of evil, the feminine counterpart of Loki.

"Yes," replied Odin, eagerly; "all the gold of Asgard, our best swords, our jewelled shields! Even Sleipnir will I give you for one draught of the precious water!"

"These things will not buy what you desire," said Mimir; "*wisdom can be gained only by suffering and sacrifice.* Would you give one of your eyes for wisdom?"

A cloud came over the bold face of Odin, and he pondered long. Finally he said slowly, "I will give one of my eyes, and I will suffer whatever else is necessary, if I may thereby gain the wisdom I need."

No one ever knew all that Odin suffered and learned in that mysterious valley. Some say that he really gave one of his eyes in return for the drink from Mimir's well. But as nothing is said of that in the old song called "Odin's Rune-song," and as the fact of his being one-eyed is not mentioned in some of the oldest poems, it seems doubtful whether that sacrifice was required of him. Odin says in his Rune-song : —

> I know that I hung
> on a wind-rocked tree,
> nine whole nights,
> with a spear wounded
> and to Odin offered,
> myself to myself;

on that tree,
of which no one knows
from what root it springs.

Bread no one gave me,
nor a horn of drink;
downward I peered,
to runes applied myself,
wailing learnt them,
then fell down thence.

Potent songs nine
from the famed son, I learned,
of Bölthorn, Bestla's sire,
and a draught obtained
of the precious mead
drawn from Odhrærir.

Then I began to bear fruit,
and to know many things,
to grow and well thrive:
word by word
I sought out words,
fact by fact
I sought out facts.[1]

---

[1] From Odin's Rune-song in Thorpe's translation of Sæmund's Edda.

THE BINDING OF THE WOLF.

ODIN returned to Asgard after a long absence, and all noticed that he looked more grave and majestic than ever. He spoke to no one but Frigga,[1] his wife, of the wonderful things he had seen and heard. Frigga never revealed what was told her in confidence.

Loki was away when Odin returned; and the latter at once took steps to place the children of the treacherous god and the witch of the Iron-wood where they could do no harm.

The children were worthy of their parents. One was a wolf, Fenrir, not yet fully grown; him Odin had brought to Asgard and given in charge of Tyr,[2] one of the strongest and bravest of the Æsir. Another was a dangerous serpent; and he was put into the river, Ocean, that surrounded Midgard, the world of men. As soon as he touched the bottom of the sea he began to grow, and grew so fast that before long he reached entirely around Midgard; and his tail, finding no other place, grew down his throat. He was called the Midgard serpent from that time forth. But more dreadful in ap-

[1] Frigg is the usual form.

[2] Son of Odin — one-armed god of war.

pearance than either of these monsters was the third. She had the form of a woman, but the hard heart of her mother, the witch of the Iron-wood; and half her body was of a deathly white color, so that no one could bear to look upon her. Odin sent her to Urd, guardian of the fountain under the third root of the World Tree, and ruler of all the realms of the dead. She made this dreadful being queen of the world of torture under Niflheim.

Loki's last two children were well disposed of, for the present, at least; but the wolf, Fenrir, kept growing stronger and fiercer each day; and Tyr, powerful as he was, found it no easy matter to control him. After consulting together, the gods decided to bind him with an iron chain.

There was a smithy in Asgard, with the best facilities for making all kinds of metal things, such as chains, swords, shields, and axes. And in this smithy the gods forged a chain larger and stronger than any that had ever been seen in Asgard. They took it to Fenrir and asked him to amuse them by showing his strength.

Fenrir was very proud of his strength; and as soon as he saw the chain, he knew he could easily break it. So he let them bind him, standing quietly as they did so. When they had finished, he stretched his limbs, and the chain instantly broke in several places. The gods pretended to consider it a good joke, and praised the wolf for his strength, saying they would try the game again some day.

They now realized that to make a chain strong enough to bind the wolf was likely to prove no easy task. This time the most skilful workers in metal were secured, and they did their best to make the second chain the strongest that could possibly be forged. When it was finished, all declared that nothing like it had ever been seen in all the nine worlds.

They went to Fenrir as before; but when he saw them bringing a chain so heavy that it took several gods merely to drag it along the ground, his suspicions were aroused. He refused to be bound. Then they appealed to his pride till his strength swelled within him; and, eager to show his power, he let them wind the chain around till his whole body was covered with iron links. Then he rolled on the ground, and stretched his huge limbs, and the bonds burst as though made of some brittle metal. The gods dissembled their feelings as best they could, and praised the strength and courage of the wolf more than ever.

Odin, with his great wisdom, realized how important it was that Fenrir should be bound. Finding that Asgard could not produce a chain strong enough for that purpose, he sent Skirnir to the home of the dark elves to get one. For great as were the gods, the elves and giants knew more about some things than they did.

And indeed, the dark elves must have been very wise and skilful to have made the chain which they gave Skirnir. How they managed to get the materials of which it was composed is a mystery; for it was made of six things seldom seen in Asgard or Midgard, — namely: the footfalls of a cat, the beard of a woman, the roots of a mountain, the sinews of a bear, the breath of a fish, and the spittle of birds. One could believe almost anything of a chain made of such things. It is no wonder that it was as soft and smooth as a silken string, and that its strength was greater than that of any chain made since the nine worlds were formed.

Skirnir did his errand very quickly, considering the long distance he had to go; and happy were the gods when he returned with the delicate, silken string. They felt sure of success now; for things made by the dark elves always possessed wonderful properties.

In order to disarm the suspicions of Fenrir, the gods planned an excursion to a rocky island, pretending that the sole object of the trip was amusement. The amusement was to consist mainly in trials of strength. Fenrir went with them. Had he discovered any chain, he would have suspected foul play; but there was nothing of the kind to be seen.

As soon as they reached the island, the sports began. They ran races, leaped over barriers, shot with bows, wrestled, and, in short, did all those things that test men's strength and skill. After the trials were ended and the victors had been crowned, they sat on the grass near Fenrir, talking and jesting.

One of the gods then drew from his bosom the magic chain, and handing it to his neighbor, said, "They say this cord is stronger than it looks. See if you can break it." The one to whom it was given tried in vain ; and then with a jest he passed it to the god next him, and so it went the rounds.

When all had tried and failed, Skirnir said, as though struck by a sudden thought, "Let Fenrir try. He has strength in breaking chains, if he can do nothing else."

So one of the gods held up the cord, saying, "Would you like to try your strength on this little string, Fenrir? Perhaps you will scorn to be bound by so slight a thing ; but it is too strong for our hands to break."

The wolf refused the trial, for he suspected treachery. Then they taunted him, saying that only a coward would refuse to be bound by such a cobweb. Their taunts stirred Fenrir's pride ; and he finally agreed to let them bind the chain about him, if one of their number would put his right hand into his jaws while it was being done, as a pledge of their good faith.

Upon this the gods looked at one another in dismay. But after an instant's pause, Tyr, well knowing what the result would be, stepped up to the wolf, and thrust

his right hand into his jaws, saying, with a laugh, " You
see it is only a joke, Fenrir!"

The wolf let them bind him; and when the magic
cord was tightly around, the gods moved away, all but
Tyr, for they knew the struggle would be terrible.

The monster now stretched his limbs; and finding
that the more he struggled the tighter grew the string,
he bit Tyr's hand off at the wrist and then rolled on
the ground, rending the air with his howls of rage and
despair. When he had worn himself out with his desperate struggles, the gods secured him and took him
back to Asgard.

Odin had him carried to a dark cave, on a rocky
island, in the regions of torture below Niflheim.[1] He
was chained to a rock that was sunk far into the earth,
and his jaws were kept open by a sword that was thrust
into them so that the hilt stood in the lower jaw and
the point in the roof of his mouth. From his jaws
flowed a poisonous river. There he would remain
chained until Ragnarok, the Twilight of the Gods,
should come.

Brave Tyr, by his sacrifice, had saved Asgard from
a dangerous foe.

[1] Rydberg describes the regions of torture in his Teutonic Mythology.

THE JUDGMENT HALL OF THE DEAD.

EACH day Odin and the other gods rode over
Bifrost, going towards the south, and went down to
the lower world. Near the southern end of the celestial bridge was the well that watered the third root of
Yggdrasil. An old book says that the waters of this
well were so "holy that everything that is put in the
well becomes as white as the membrane between the
egg and the eggshell." The roots of Yggdrasil were
continually sprinkled with its waters, and were as white
as silver in consequence. Two swans of purest white,
the parents of all the swans that ever have been, glided
over its surface ; and its edge, like that of Mimir's well,
was thickly overlaid with gold.

Urd, the great norn who was queen of the world of
the dead, dwelt near the well with her two sisters.
Multitudes of messengers and attendants stood ready
to do her bidding ; for her realms were vast, her power
extending even to the dark region under Niflheim. All
beings who died in Midgard came first to the great
judgment hall near her well. And it was to meet them
there, and with Urd to pass judgment upon them, that
the gods crossed each day the trembling bridge and

came to the lower world.   Thor, the thunder-god, could not pass over the bridge, because his heavy iron chariot would have injured it ; so he was obliged to ford three rivers on his way.

The great judgment hall was a solemn place, and the decisions pronounced there, whether gentle or severe, were always just.   Mortals who had been very wicked were sent to the world of torture.   Those who had died on the field of battle were claimed by Odin, the Allfather, or by Freyia, a Van-goddess who lived in Asgard with the Æsir.   Odin sent his maidens, the Valkyries, to choose the heroes on the battle-field, and to conduct them to Asgard.   They went to his great palace of Valhalla ; and there they feasted and fought each day, that they might be ready to do battle with the powers of evil when Ragnarok, the Twilight of the Gods, should come.[1]   Freyia united again lovers who had been faithful unto death.   Mortals whose lives had been peaceful and pure went to a home prepared for them by Urd, in a land where the fields stretched green and beautiful, and where it was always summer.

[1] Frey's sister, a Van-goddess. Half of the slain in battle belonged to her.

BALDUR AND LOKI.

NONE of the gods stood so high in the judgment hall of the dead as Baldur. While he was not famed as a fighter, or noted for his strength, his pure heart and righteous life made his judgment so clear that his decisions were absolutely just, and once spoken were never questioned.

Besides being a perfect judge, Baldur had other qualities that made every one love him, even the strong and fierce. He was so full of kindness and sympathy that wherever he went the sun shone more brightly, and joy filled all hearts. From the first his life had been blameless, and his one aim had been to make others happy. The loveliness of his character was expressed in his face and in his form; he was the most beautiful of all the gods: indeed, they often called him Baldur the Beautiful; and in Midgard, men named the whitest flower they could find, Baldur's brow.

But dearly loved as he was, Baldur had one deadly enemy, — the false, vindictive Loki. Loki secretly hated all the gods, but none so much as Baldur. His fierce jealousy was stirred because Baldur held such a high place in Asgard. He hated him as the darkness hates the light, and as evil abhors good; and all his plots and schemes tended to one end, — the destruction of this hated being. He had long hoped to bring about in some way the downfall of Odin and the ruin of Asgard; but first he would kill Baldur, for well he knew that nothing would cause such universal grief as his death.

BALDUR'S DREAMS.

Baldur, the beloved of the gods, had grown sad. His palace, the " Hall-of-broad-shining-splendor," [1] no longer gave him pleasure, and Nanna, his wife, could not comfort him. His voice was not heard in the council hall of the gods. Finally, after suffering long in silence, he confided to Odin and Frigga the cause of his sorrow. Every night, for a long while, he had been tormented by dreams which told him that the day of his death was not far distant, that he must leave the home he loved so well, to dwell in the under-world, apart from all his brethren. This thought made him so sad that the most joyous sights and sounds could not drive away his melancholy.

Odin at once called a council of all the gods and goddesses, and after conferring together, they sent some of their number to consult wise giants and other beings who knew more of the future than they themselves knew. All said that Baldur must die.

Then it was determined that from every living creature, and from all plants and metals, the oath not to harm Baldur should be exacted. Frigga received their

[1] Breidablik.

oaths; and for days Asgard was thronged with the multitude of beings who came to take the solemn oath; until, finally, all had sworn.

But even this did not satisfy Odin. He resolved to go to the lower world and there seek information about the fate of his son. Sleipnir was saddled; and the All-father took the same road that he had travelled when he visited the realms of Mimir in search of wisdom. Again he crossed the celestial bridge, going towards the north, and passed again the shining castle of Heimdall, the sleepless watchman. But this time Sleipnir bore him swiftly through the dark ice region and the gloomy land of the mountain giants.

As he was going toward the south, a dog met him, having come evidently from the cave near Mount Hvergelmir. The breast of the dog was bloody, and so were his throat and his lower jaw. He barked furiously at Odin, and howled long after he had passed; but the Allfather rode on, not heeding him.

In the eastern part of Mimir's realm, near the home of Delling, the elf of the dawn, Odin came to a dense forest [1] that he could not remember having seen before.

---

[1] The forest and castle have been introduced into the Baldur myth on Rydberg's authority. Mimir saved some pure mortals at the time of an impending catastrophe, and placed them in this castle. Baldur came, after his death, and ruled over them. After the destruction of the world, at Ragnarök, Baldur was to rule, and these mortals, who had long served him,

Yet the locality was familiar to him, and he knew that a little farther to the east was the grave of the Vala,[1] whom he wished to consult. After penetrating for a long distance into the silent depths of the wood, he came to a wall, higher than the one around Asgard. However, Sleipnir was not daunted by this obstacle; and in an instant Odin found himself in a large garden, from the midst of which rose a castle of singular beauty. The doors stood hospitably open: evidently no enemies were anticipated in this charmed spot, protected by forest and wall. The Allfather dismounted and entered.

Tall men and fair women walked about the castle, or talked together in small groups; and there were preparations as for some honored guest whose coming was expected. At the upper end of the hall was a throne of gold, and near it benches, strewn with rings

were to re-people the earth. These lines from the lay of Vafthrûdnir in Sæmund's Edda refer to the subject: —

> "What mortals will live,
>   when the great Fimbul-winter
>   shall from men have passed?"
>   Vafthrûdnir.
> "Lîf and Lîfthrasir;
>   but they will be concealed
>   in Hoddmimir's holt.
>   The morning dews
>   they will have for food.
>   From them shall men be born."

[1] A prophetess.

and ornaments; while on the table the mead stood ready; but it was covered with a shield.

As Odin entered, a graceful youth came forward, saying reverently, "Are you the good king, and the wise, that Mimir has long promised us? You see that everything is in readiness, and your subjects await you with impatience."

And Odin answered, "I am indeed the king of a fair realm, but not your king. What is the name of him who is to rule over you?"

And the youth replied, "Mimir has not told us his name; but we know he is to come erelong; and he will be so noble and so pure that we shall all love him and serve him gladly."

Odin sighed, thinking of Baldur. After talking a little with the inhabitants of the castle, the Allfather left them, and made his way out of the forest.

Upon reaching the grave of the Vala, Odin chanted a magic song, compelling her to rise and answer him. She rose, and with a deathlike voice, said, "What man is this, to me unknown, who has for me increased an irksome course? I have with snow been decked, by rain beaten, and with dew moistened; long have I been dead."

Odin did not give his real name, but said, "Vegtam is my name; I am Valtam's son. Tell me what I wish to know of the realms of death: from earth I call on you. For whom are those benches strewn o'er with rings, and those costly couches o'erlaid with gold?"

And the Vala answered, "Mead stands for Baldur brewed; over the bright potion a shield is laid; but the Æsir race are in despair. By compulsion I have spoken; I will now be silent."

Then Odin spoke again: "Be not silent, Vala; I will question you until I know all. I must yet know who will Baldur's slayer be; who will kill the son of Odin?"

The Vala said, "Hódur[1] will thither his glorious brother send; he will the slayer of Baldur be; he will kill the son of Odin. By compulsion I have spoken; I will now be silent."

However, Odin kept on questioning the Vala, until he asked something that revealed his true character; and she said, "Not Vegtam are you, as I before believed; you are Odin, lord of men! Homeward ride; Odin, and exult! Nevermore shall man thus visit me, until Ragnarök, the Twilight of the Gods, have come."

As she said this, the Vala sank back into the earth. And Odin rode again to Asgard, little comforted by what he had learned in the lower world.

---

[1] Said to be blind. He may have represented winter, the slayer of summer.

THE MISTLETOE.

It seemed as though death could not come near Baldur now; for all beings had sworn that they would not hurt him. The purest of the gods was surely saved. One day he chanced to be hit by an arrow; and, had another been in his place, the wound would have been fatal; but when the arrow touched him, it was blunted, and he was not hurt. Seeing this, some of the gods begged him to stand as a mark, while they amused themselves by hurling things at him; stones, spears, arrows and swords, — nothing could harm him.

Loki passed by as the Æsir were enjoying this game, and fierce jealousy filled his heart when he saw Baldur so calm in a position that would have meant death to any other being. Taking the form of a decrepit old woman, Loki went to the mansion of Frigga, and asked alms. Frigga gave the seeming beggar something, and then asked what the gods were doing as she crossed the plains of Ida. The woman replied that they were throwing stones and weapons at Baldur, who stood there, unhurt.

"Ah!" exclaimed the queen, "they cannot harm him now, whatever his dreams may be, for I have exacted an oath from all things!"

"What!" said the woman, in a weak, shaky voice. "Have *all* things sworn not to harm him?"

"Yes," replied Frigga; "all things." Then she added carelessly, "There was one little shrub, the mistletoe, that grows on the eastern side of Valhalla, too weak to do any harm. I did not exact an oath from that."

Had Frigga been watching the old woman narrowly, she would have seen a look of triumph come into her face as she heard these words. But the queen of the gods scarcely noticed her, so absorbed was she in thinking of her dear son. And the beggar crept quietly out of the palace, and disappeared behind a clump of bushes.

In a few moments Loki was talking gayly with the gods on the plains of Ida, and congratulating Baldur on his ability to stand unhurt amid a shower of weapons.

After dark, when all Asgard was asleep, a form might have been seen creeping stealthily towards the eastern side of Valhalla. It was Loki. When he found the slender mistletoe, he pulled it up by the roots and hid it in his bosom. From that time it never left him; and he was continually planning to get some skilful maker of weapons to form from it an arrow fatal to Baldur.

LOKI MAKES TROUBLE BETWEEN THE ARTISTS[1] AND THE GODS.

Loki once cut off the beautiful hair of Sif, Thor's wife. And when Thor found out that Loki was the culprit, he threatened to crush every bone in his body if he did not repair the mischief he had done. Loki promised to do this, for he feared Thor. He went at once to the sons of Ivaldi for help. They were famous artists, these sons of Ivaldi. Many were the weapons and ornaments they had made for the gods. They quickly spun some golden hair for Sif. This wonderful hair grew to her head, becoming like her own hair, except that it was gold.

Besides this they sent a spear to Odin, and a ship to Frey. The spear was sure to hit the mark each time ; and the ship, called Skidbladnir, could be folded up like a napkin and put into the pocket when not in use : it would always have fair winds.

It has been told how Odin, on his journey to Mimir's well, passed near the singular hall of the dwarf Sindri and his brothers. One day when Loki was near there, it occurred to him that it would be an easy matter to

---

[1] The artists, the productive forces of vegetation.

stir up jealousy between the two sets of artists. Perhaps, too, he could, at the same time, make trouble between them and the gods.

One of Sindri's brothers was outside the castle as Loki came near; and the latter at once began to talk with him about the making of beautiful and curious objects. Loki described the wonderful gifts the sons of Ivaldi had sent the gods by him, and then said, "I will wager my head that you cannot make, you and your brothers, three treasures as good as those I have just described!"

The dwarf was angry at this disparagement of their skill, and hurried into the hall to tell Sindri of Loki's wager. Loki went in after him, and repeated what he had said, adding, that if they would make the gifts, the gods themselves should be the judges, and pronounce upon the merits of the rival artists.

They went to the smithy, which was in another part of the castle. The heat from the great furnace was so intense that even Loki, who loved fire, could hardly bear it. Sindri took down a pigskin that was hanging on the wall, and putting it into the furnace, told his brother Brok to blow the bellows, and not stop blowing until he took the pigskin out.

Loki stepped behind some iron-work, and instantly a fly appeared upon the hand of Brok as he was blowing the bellows, and stung him badly; but he bore the pain, and did not stop blowing. Very soon Sindri drew from the furnace a boar with golden bristles.

Next, Sindri put some gold into the furnace, giving his brother the same directions. This time the fly settled upon Brok's neck, and stung him so that he lifted his shoulders, but still kept on blowing. The result was a ring.

The next time, Sindri put iron into the furnace; and as Brok was blowing, the fly buzzed angrily, and settling between his eyes, stung him so severely on the eyelid that the blood ran down into his eye, and he could not see. He stopped blowing for an instant and brushed the fly away. A hammer came out this time; but the handle was a little too short.

The three treasures were now finished, and Loki left the dwarfs, naming a day for them to meet him in Asgard. He set out at once for the home of the sons of Ivaldi. One of these artists, Thiassi, who was as large as a giant, and who was said to have great skill as a magician, went with him to Asgard. The treasures made by the last-named artists were already in the possession of the god.

It was a fair morning in the beautiful city when the judgment was to be pronounced. Gladsheim glittered in the sun. Upon its marble walls were pictured the wonders of the nine worlds, and the mighty deeds of gods and heroes in the earliest times. Mimir's mysterious valley, Urd's pure fountain, Mount Hvergelmir with its ice-cold spring, — all could be seen on those vast walls. And there, too, were Surt's fiery dales below the realms of Urd, the dark, misty regions of Niflheim, and even the world of torture with its stagnant sea. In other pictures lived again the strange beings and huge, uncouth monsters of the ancient world.

The great hall of Gladsheim was to be the scene of the judgment. There was Odin's throne. Over it rose the arch of Bifrost, so like the real bridge that it sent forth fitful flames. Back of the throne was a golden tree, representing Yggdrasil, the World Tree. The trembling leaves flashed in the sunlight that streamed in through the eastern openings. Sif, with her golden hair, sat near a table in the centre of the hall. And upon the table lay Odin's spear and Frey's ship, made by the sons of Ivaldi.

The hour had come, and all eyes were turned toward the wide door, as Loki entered, accompanied by the enormous Thiassi. Loki's eyes sparkled with malicious pleasure ; and, after making his reverence to Odin, he began talking gayly with the other gods. Thiassi came in awkwardly, as though unused to scenes of such grandeur and beauty. He saluted Odin and the greater gods, and then seated himself near Sif, who tried in vain to make him talk with her.

In a few moments, two diminutive figures appeared at the great entrance, and with them a large boar whose golden bristles dazzled the eyes. One of the dwarfs led the boar, while the other carried a small hammer. They paid their respects to Odin and the other gods in a peculiar, jerky manner, and then stood looking about with eager, inquisitive faces.

Odin rose, and said, in a deep voice, "We are here to decide upon the comparative skill of two sets of artists. They are both very skilful, and we are indebted to both for many rare and valuable gifts. It will be a difficult task to judge rightly, and we regret that Loki has made a judgment necessary. He, however, has promised to forfeit his head to Sindri and his brothers should the decision be in their favor."

He paused a moment, and all looked at Loki's head on which the stiff, red hair gleamed like fire; a smile lurked about his treacherous mouth, and his eyes twinkled.

Odin went on: "Let Thiassi state the peculiar properties and special merits of his work and that of his brothers; and then Sindri shall follow him, and speak of his gifts."

Thiassi rose up, a sullen, defiant look in his face; evidently he was forced to play a part ill-suited to him. Pointing to Sif, he said, "There is Thor's wife; you can all see her golden hair; it needs no praise." Taking up the spear that lay on the table, he went on, "This is a good spear; it never misses the mark."

He next took from the table what seemed to be a white napkin; but as he held it, it bloomed and spread, until a ship appeared that grew larger and larger while he talked. "This ship is like no other," he said; "it can be made small enough to be carried in the pocket, or large enough to hold many men; it always has a fair wind."

Thiassi did not raise his eyes as he talked, but uttered every sentence as though it cost him an effort, making long pauses between. When he had finished speaking, he put the ship — which again looked like a napkin — upon the table, and with a sigh of relief sat down.

Sindri then came forward, his small, bright eyes peering everywhere, and his face eager and excited. His brother stood by his side, watching him intently, and imitating all his gestures. Sindri pointed to the boar, saying: "This boar is worthy of higher praise than I can give him. You see how his golden bristles flash in the sunlight; but in the darkest night their brightness is the same. On this boar Frey can ride through Niflheim itself and still have day; and so swift is he, that Sleipnir with his eight legs cannot outrun him. He can fly through the air, or skim over the sea, as his rider wills." As he said this, Sindri looked keenly at

Thiassi, as though searching in his face for a look of conscious defeat.

He next drew from his bosom a ring,[1] and as he held it up in the sunlight, all could see the stones of many colors that sparkled in the setting of yellow gold. After gazing upon it for a moment as though fascinated by the beautiful object, Sindri spoke: "Were this ring merely what it seems, it would need no words of mine; but it has a most marvellous property. Every ninth night, eight rings of equal size and beauty drop from it. There is not another treasure like it in all the nine worlds!" And Sindri put the ring down slowly, as though loath to part with it.

He then took the hammer from his brother. As he raised it, that it might be seen by all, it grew larger and larger, until the strength of both dwarfs was needed merely to hold it upright on the floor. With a look of triumph, Sindri cried: "This mighty hammer, called Miollnir, will be more useful to Thor when he meets the frost giants than his wife's golden hair! It will strike whatever it is aimed at, without fail, let the thing be large or small; and it will always return to the hand that flings it. Besides, it can be easily carried; for it can be made so small as to go into the pocket." He glanced at Loki as he added, "To be sure, the handle is a little too short."

[1] The ring Draupnir, said to represent fertility.

As Sindri finished speaking, he and his brother looked around exultingly. Thiassi's face was expressionless, except for a haughty curl of the lip.

After a short pause, Odin rose, saying, "Let Sif come here, and let all the treasures be brought. We will examine them carefully and then pronounce our judgment."

While the gods were examining and consulting, the dwarfs watched them intently, their quick glance going from one to another; but Thiassi sat motionless, his head buried in his hands, apparently half asleep.

After a long consultation, silence was commanded. As Odin rose, every eye was fastened upon him. "It has been a hard task," he began, "to decide between such wonderful and useful gifts; but the decision must be given. We consider that the gifts made by the dwarfs, Sindri and his brothers, surpass in some respects those made by the sons of Ivaldi." Then turning to Loki, he added, "Loki, you have forfeited your head; defend yourself as best you can!"

As Odin pronounced the judgment, a look of disappointment came into Thiassi's countenance, followed by an expression of fierce hatred, and bitter words escaped through his closed teeth. But the faces of the two dwarfs beamed with triumph and delight.

Sindri instantly sprang towards Loki, crying: "Your head belongs to me, you crafty god! Never again shall

you turn yourself into a fly to spoil the work of Sindri!
Your red hair will make bristles for my next boar!"
He tried to seize Loki, while he drew from beneath his
mantle a large knife.

The nimble god slipped from his grasp, however,
and was instantly out of the hall and speeding like the
wind over the plains of Ida.

Sindri called for help. Then Thor, laughing mightily
at the frantic rage of the dwarf, took up his hammer,
and cried in a voice of thunder, "Come back, you coward, or I'll try my hammer on you! Remember, it
always hits!" The sound of Thor's voice produced a
quick effect upon the runaway. He stopped, and came
slowly back to the palace.

"Try your wits, now your heels have failed you,"
said Thor.

As the dwarf again approached Loki, prepared to cut
off his head, the latter cried, "The head is yours, but
not the neck!" Sindri stopped, and looked question-
ingly at the gods.

And they all said, "Loki is right! Not the neck!"

"I am cheated," yelled the angry dwarf. And
quickly seizing his brother's awl, he sprang toward
Loki, and in an instant had sewed his lips together
with a stout thread. Thereupon he and his brother
left the hall. Thiassi was nowhere to be seen. He
had disappeared while Sindri and Loki were disputing.

Well had Loki succeeded in stirring up jealousy and hatred where all had been peace and good-will. Thiassi had left the great palace, full of rage against the gods, and with plans for revenge already seething in his brain; while Sindri and his brother were equally angry at the loss of their wager and at the mirth of the gods at their expense. Besides, the bitterest jealousy was now aroused between the two sets of artists.

HOW THIASSI CAPTURED LOKI.

ODIN, Loki, and another god set out upon a journey. The road lay through thickets, where they could
scarcely make their way, and up steep hills; so that
fatigue and hunger at last compelled them to stop.
They threw themselves down on the edge of a field
where some oxen and cows were grazing. Loki, whose
appetite was always keen, suggested that one of the
oxen would make a good meal. In a few moments the
creature was captured and killed. While Loki was pre-
paring the meat for boiling, the other gods brought
boughs and small trees to make the fire. Then they
retired into the shade.

Loki watched the fire with delight. The red flames
sent their forked tongues up around the huge iron
kettle, the steam rose in clouds, and the water hissed
as the pot boiled over. He laughed gleefully, and
cried, "Burn, fire, hot and high, and cook us a dinner
fit for gods!" And he threw on more wood.

Soon it was time for the meat to be done. So Loki
found a forked stick and fished out a piece, which he
examined and tasted. To his astonishment, it was as
raw as when first put in. He stared at the pot, and at

the fire, with a look of bewilderment. Then he piled on wood till the fire roared.

In a little while he again tried the meat, but with no better success: it was still raw. The fooler of others, the knave among the gods, was at his wits' end. He gazed at the kettle, exclaiming, "The evil powers are at work! The frost giants have got into the fire!"

Just then he heard a mocking laugh, which seemed to come from above. And looking up, he saw an enormous eagle that returned his gaze with a steady stare that nearly put him out of countenance; for the eagle's eyes shone like stars.

Finally the bird spoke: "Well, friend Loki, why doesn't your meat cook? You seem to lack skill, or else bad luck attends you. Give me my share of the feast, and the meat will be done soon enough."

Loki was already out of patience, and the words of the eagle made him angry. "Stop your jeering," he cried, "or you shall feel the might of an Asa!"

Then the mocking laugh sounded again; and the eagle said, "Keep your threats, Loki, for those whom you can reach. You are 'little pot, soon hot,' unlike your big kettle there."

The god was now thoroughly enraged; but knowing himself to be helpless, he controlled his anger, and said mildly, "Suppose we stop our jesting and get the meat cooked. Take your portion, if it will help matters. The meat is bewitched."

Upon this, the eagle swooped down, and seizing a leg and two shoulders of the ox, — which might certainly be called the lion's share, — was about to fly off with them, when Loki, seeing what he had done, quickly seized a long pole that was lying near, and struck him a hard blow. But, alas for Loki! The pole stuck fast to the eagle's back, and the other end would not leave Loki's hands. The bird sailed up into the air, carrying with him the astonished god. He soon lowered his flight, so that Loki was dragged over trees and sharp rocks till he howled with pain.

After a while the eagle, tired from carrying so heavy a burden, stopped on the crest of a hill and looked around at his captive. The latter was nearly dead with fright and pain; but he got his breath in a moment, and began to beg for mercy.

The bird listened to him, and laughed his mocking laugh again, as he said, "Don't you know me yet, Loki? Do you forget your friends so soon?"

Loki stared for a moment, and then cried, "You are Thiassi!"

"Of course I am Thiassi," replied the bird. "I did not think you could be so easily deceived. But I have no desire to harm you. It is the other gods I wish to reach, — those who pronounced in favor of the dwarfs.

Dearly shall they pay for the insult done to us! They shall yet feel the edge of the fatal sword!" and the eagle's eyes flashed.

"How can I serve you?" said Loki. "Do not count me an enemy, I beg of you."

"I know you of old, Loki," replied Thiassi; "and I know that mischief delights you whether the victim be friend or foe. The game I am going to play will be after your own heart. Iduna,[1] as you may remember, is a kinswoman of mine. I saw her the day the judgment was pronounced, — the first time in years. I fancy she must at times weary of the charming monotony of Asgard, and long for a peep at her giant kin. I intend to gratify her unspoken wish. In so doing I shall cause some discomfort to my enemies, the fair gods. Their brows will soon be wrinkled and their forms bent, if the charming Iduna, with her golden apples, leaves them."

At the picture of the happy gods careworn and wrinkled, Loki laughed aloud, forgetting his recent pain. "Thiassi, your plan is excellent, and I will help you carry it out!" he cried; "but in return promise to do one thing for me. It will hurt your foes more than the loss of Iduna."

"Speak;" said Thiassi; "I will do anything for re-venge."

[1] Idun or Idunn, usual form; the goddess of early spring.

"To injure the gods most deeply," said Loki, "one must hurt Baldur. He is their idol. They worship him, as though he were a higher kind of being — even Odin does. I do not share this enthusiasm, as you may imagine. So far as I can remember, I have never found any one in all the nine worlds to admire; and I hate their meek Baldur as much as they love him. Some time ago their favorite had bad dreams, and had them so repeatedly that Father Odin and Mother Frigga, becoming alarmed for their darling, called a council of the gods, consulted wise giants, and finally made all living creatures, and even the plants and metals, swear not to harm Baldur.

"Not satisfied with this, Odin visited the lower world and consulted a Vala, long since dead, concerning his son's fate. I overheard him telling Frigga about his journey. He rode on Sleipnir. When he was near the cave that leads to the world of torture, a dog met him, and barked furiously, — a bad sign, I believe. I lost what came next. But at last he reached the grave of the Vala, who, I assure you, was not pleased to be disturbed after her long sleep under the dew and the snow. She told Odin that a place was being made ready for his son in the lower world. I did not hear all, but I am convinced that Odin got little comfort from his journey.

"This meek Baldur now parades his superiority by

standing up as a mark for the Æsir. He thinks himself safe now; but I happen to possess a little secret of great importance. Mother Frigga, in her innocence, confided it to me, taking me for a beggar-woman. When she made all creatures swear not to harm Baldur, there was one she neglected because it was so weak, so powerless to harm any one. It was the little shrub mistletoe that grew on the eastern side of Valhalla. Of course, I at once secured the plant, and here it is." And Loki drew from his bosom the withered mistletoe.

"Now for my plot, friend Thiassi! From this weak plant, you, with your wonderful skill, can make an arrow that will kill the fair-faced Baldur, the darling of the gods."

Thiassi pondered a moment, and then said, "I would not do so much to please you. You are in my power, and I can compel you to help me whether you will or not. But I like your plot. Give me the mistletoe. The arrow I make shall be deadly; for it shall be poisoned by hate. I have already made a fatal sword whose edge the Æsir shall feel some day. Mimir, the wise, took it from me while I slept. I know not where it is; but it will surely fulfil the end for which it was made."

Before they parted, it was arranged that Loki should entice Iduna outside the walls of Asgard, so that Thiassi could carry her off to Jötunheim. And Thiassi, as he flew towards the north, bore with him the withered mistletoe from which he was to make the fatal arrow.

THIASSI CARRIES OFF IDUNA.

Iduna was sitting in her garden one afternoon, when Loki wandered in, and threw himself down on a low seat. All the gods came often to see Iduna. It was a charming spot, this garden, with its fountains and bowers, and Iduna was a lovely goddess. But the gods had another reason for coming, — they came to get Iduna's apples.

These apples were the most delicious fruit. They were golden in color, just touched with red; and one seemed to be eating whatever he liked best in the world when he tasted them. And there was something still more wonderful about them. Whoever ate them, if old, grew young, and if tired, felt as fresh as though just awaking from sleep. Because of these virtues, the Æsir prized them above all their treasures.

As Loki sat there, Thor, the strong god of thunder, came for refreshment after fighting with the giants in Jötunheim. Baldur the Beautiful came; for even he needed to taste the wondrous fruit. In a moment Tyr walked up, strong and cheerful in spite of the loss of his right hand. Later, came Frigga and some of the other goddesses. And all talked pleasantly together as they strolled about among the trees, or rested in the shady bowers.

Loki chuckled as he thought to himself, "How will mighty Thor feel when his hand is too weak to fling the hammer at the giants? and how will Frigga look, when she can no longer stand erect, queen of the gods, but must totter about, a bent old woman? Oh, it will be rare sport!"

The gods came and went, and the shadows lengthened, but still Loki lingered. When at last he was alone with Iduna, he said carelessly, "Let me see one of your apples a moment; I wish to examine it." After looking at it critically, he smelt of it and tasted it. Then he said, in a decided tone, "Yes, it is as I thought; those apples are much finer!"

Iduna looked at him with an expression of bewilderment.

He continued: "The gold is brighter, and the red a more beautiful shade; and the flavor is beyond that of anything I have ever tasted. I would never have believed there were apples better than yours in all the nine worlds, had I not seen and tasted them myself."

As Loki talked, amazement and anxiety were pictured on Iduna's face; and when he finished, she burst out, — "Why, Loki! what do you mean? There cannot be apples better than mine! All the gods say so, — even Odin himself; and he has been everywhere."

"So the gods say, but how can they prove it?" said Loki, smiling. "I have seen finer ones and have eaten them. They grow just beyond the wall and river of Asgard, in a grove. No one would ever think of looking there for apples. I found them by chance, the other day, when searching for something I had lost."

"O Loki!" cried Iduna, with tears in her eyes, "I cannot bear to think there are apples better than mine. I wonder if they are also apples of youth?"

"As to that I cannot say," replied the god; "I only know that I was quite exhausted when I came upon them, and the first taste made me feel as fresh as a lark. So I presume they surpass your apples in their youth-giving and refreshing qualities as well as in other things. However," he added, seeing Iduna's look of distress, "you need not be alarmed. I know how sad a thing it would be for you to lose your position as sole possessor of the wonderful fruit. And so, out of consideration for you, I have spoken to no one of my discovery. You, charming Iduna, who have always been so gracious and so generous in dispensing your treasure, you alone must have the new golden apples!"

"How kind you are, Loki!" said Iduna, the tears still in her eyes; "won't you get me some of them, so that I can see for myself how much better they are? It seems as though I could not wait!"

"Let me think," said Loki, meditatively; "I must

start for Midgard to-night. How can I manage it?" Then in a moment, he added: "I should not have time to get the apples and come back here with them; but this is what we can do. You go with me. I shall have time to see you safely into Asgard again; and once inside the walls, you will not mind coming home alone. Or, if you prefer, you need not go outside at all. I will get the apples while you wait inside. You can decide which you would rather do when we get there."

The unsuspecting Iduna prepared to go with Loki. She threw over her shoulders a light green mantle, her flower-embroidered robe showing gayly below it. Then she said, "I wonder whether I had better hide my apples, or take them with me."

"Oh, take them," Loki replied, "and then you won't be worrying about them."

They started off, Iduna half frightened and half pleased at the prospect of so long a trip ; for she rarely left her own home, and had not been beyond the walls for years.

"I wonder what Bragi will say if he comes back and does not find me," she murmured. "I hope I shall get home before dark!" And she was almost ready to turn back. But Loki was very gay, and his jests and stories soon made her forget her fears.

After a long walk — and gods walk much faster than mortals — they reached the walls of the city.

"Now," said Loki, "which will you do? stay here or go with me? It makes no difference, unless you would like to see the apples growing; and possibly you may not fancy being left by yourself in such a lonely spot."

"I am a little afraid to stay here alone," said Iduna, "and I should like to see the apples growing. I think I will go with you. There can't be any harm in my going if it is so near."

Loki helped her over the high wall. And, strange to say, there was a curious boat just where they got down on the other side. Had Iduna been in the least suspicious she might have wondered at its being there. She did not stop to wonder, but stepped in with Loki. The boat went over the rushing river with its dangerous mists as easily as a swan crosses a smooth lake. For, in truth, it was no common boat, but one made by Thiassi for this very occasion.

As they stepped on shore, Loki pointed to a grove of trees, saying, " The apples are in there."

They went toward the grove, and soon the long rays of the afternoon sun were shut out by the trees and the thick undergrowth.

Iduna was tired, and said in a weary tone, "Is it much further, Loki?"

"No, only a little way," he replied; "but if you are tired, here is a nice mossy seat in this little opening. You can rest a few moments, while I go and get some water from the spring that bubbles out from the other side of the large rock yonder."

Iduna sat down, holding her basket of golden apples in her lap, and leaning her beautiful head against a tree. Looking up through the opening, she could see the white clouds sailing lazily in the deep blue sky. In a few moments her eyes closed, and she was fast asleep.

She was suddenly awakened by a whirring sound, and when she looked up, the blue sky had vanished, and a dark thunder cloud was coming rapidly towards the opening.

"Loki! Loki! come back!" she cried.

There was no reply, and the cloud came swiftly down. As it touched the tree-tops, a few feathers fell into Iduna's lap; and as she gazed in fear and wonder, it took the form of a large eagle with shining eyes. Iduna screamed with terror, and sank back helpless upon the mossy seat. As the eagle seized her, a small arrow dropped upon the ground near where she had been sitting.

Iduna was borne rapidly away toward Jötunheim. When the eagle was so far up that he looked no larger than a swallow, a form appeared from behind the large rock, and Loki, a look of malicious triumph in his face, picked up the mistletoe arrow.

THE GODS GROW OLD.

WHEN Bragi,[1] Iduna's husband, came home that night, his wife was not at the gate to meet him with her happy face and her golden hair. He searched for her in the garden and in the palace; he inquired of the people about the place, of her maidens, and finally of all the gods and goddesses; but no one had seen Iduna since they left her, as well and as happy as ever, in the afternoon. Thor did remember that when he left the garden, Loki sat on a low seat, half asleep.

"Thor," said Bragi, "if there is mischief, Loki is at the bottom of it! Let us find him!"

They went to Loki's home, and found him sitting by a large fire. He seemed surprised to see them, and opened his eyes wide when they told him that Iduna had disappeared.

"That is very strange!" said he; "I was the last one to leave the garden, and everything was all right then. I have seen nothing that looked suspicious near Asgard. Then, after a short pause, he added, "I did notice a large eagle as I walked home; but I do not think he came very near."

---

[1] The god of poetry; the best of skalds.

Loki seemed so innocent that they could not suspect him of knowing anything more of Iduna's whereabouts than they did.

That night and the day following, and every day, the search for Iduna was kept up; but no trace of her could be found. Great sorrow was felt throughout the city of the gods. With her, the warm summer that never left that happy home, departed, giving place to dreary November. Cold winds blew from the north, chilling the delicate flowers. A look of decay came over the hills and fields; and yellow leaves fell from the trees, leaving them bare and brown. Vines that had always borne fruit and flowers during every month of the year, rattled their lifeless stems against the tottering walls. A cold breath touched the ponds and streams, covering them with a thin coating of ice. And the birds left for the first time the summer-land of the gods and flew toward the south. The sun itself shone with a pale, sickly light, scarcely warming the blood even at noon. And the nights grew long and dark.

But if nature mourned for Iduna, the gods felt her loss still more. As long as she gave them her golden apples, weariness and old age could not touch them. Each one enjoyed the fullest life. After Iduna's going, Odin, the wise Allfather, grew older: his beard became as white as the beard of Mimir. and there was a look of sadness on his kingly features. Stately Frigga, the mother of the gods, became wrinkled and gray. Even Thor, the mighty thunder-god, showed signs of age, although his spirit was unbroken. Matters were fast becoming so desperate that Odin decided to call a council to consider what could be done to remedy the evil.

The gods and goddesses assembled, — those whose homes were far away as well as those who lived in Asgard. All came except Heimdall, who could not leave his post as guardian of the bridge Bifröst. Niörd came from his wind-blown palace by the sea, "on a strand outside of which the swans sing," in the western part of the lower world. Frey came from Alfheim, the land of the light elves; and Vidar the Silent left his lonely vine-grown home, deep in the mountains, at the call of Odin. All came, and all showed the signs of weakness and of age.

One alone was absent when the Æsir were assembled. Loki was not there. And it had been remarked that he seemed little affected by Iduna's absence. His hair gleamed red and fiery, unmixed with gray; and his restless eyes had lost none of their brightness.

All were silent until Odin arose, feeble, yet majestic, his countenance lighted by the wisdom for which he had paid so dear. "My children," he said, "Iduna has gone, and the world is growing old. The gods grow feeble. Winter winds already howl around Gladsheim. The shadow of death is upon us. Who will bring back Iduna?"

As he finished speaking, a god rose from his seat. He was one that was not often among them; for he lived far from Gladsheim, near the high wall of Asgard.

"May I speak, father Odin?" he asked.

Odin bowed his head; and he went on: "I heard in my lonely home that Iduna had gone; but it did not occur to me until recently that certain strange things I had seen could have anything to do with her disappearance. What I have to say may unravel the mystery.

"One afternoon, rather late, I climbed the high wall which is near my castle, and looked down upon the dark Asgard river. Suddenly my attention was attracted by a peculiar whirring sound, such as is made by a bird in rapid flight. Looking up, I saw an enormous eagle carrying something in his talons. I could not tell what. I watched him until he became a mere speck and at last vanished on the northern horizon. On looking down, I saw another strange sight, — a singular boat that crossed the dangerous river as easily as though it had been a common stream. Night was coming on, but I could distinguish Loki as he leaped from the boat, concealed it amid some bushes, and then quickly climbed the wall and went towards the centre of

Asgard. I do not see Loki here, and that makes it seem still more probable that he had something to do with Iduna's disappearance."

As the god sat down, Thor sprang up, the old fire flashing in his eyes. "Odin," he cried, "shall not Bragi and I seek Loki? He shall pay dearly for it, if he is the cause of all this!"

Odin gave his permission, and they left the hall. They soon came back bringing Loki, who put on an air of careless gayety, ill-suited to the occasion. Odin calmly repeated what the god had said, and Loki, finding it useless to deny that he had crossed the river with Iduna, told the whole story: how he was captured by Thiassi on the day when he suddenly disappeared while travelling with Odin and the other god, and how to save himself he had betrayed Iduna into Thiassi's hands.

Thor advanced towards the guilty god with his hammer raised; and then Loki, thoroughly frightened, begged for mercy, saying he would surely find a way to bring back Iduna, if they would only give him time.

"Loki," said Odin, sternly, "we will give you time; but if at the end of one month you do not bring her back, you shall be put to death with terrible tortures."

Loki asked for a moment's silence, that he might think of some way in which he could outwit Thiassi

This was not an easy thing to do, because the latter was a great magician. He buried his face in his hands, but in an instant looked up, saying: "I have a plan, but a disguise is needful. If Freyia will lend me her falcon plumage, I will match Thiassi with his eagle feathers." And he laughed gleefully at the thought of outwitting the great artist. Then he continued: "I know some runes by which I can change Iduna into a nut, so that I can easily bring her back. Let me go; I long to fool the giant who trailed me over the rocks and trees."

The gods looked coldly on Loki; for they saw that his chief desire was not to rescue Iduna.

A little later a falcon might have been seen flying towards the desolate mountains of Jotunheim.

LOKI BRINGS BACK IDUNA.

THE home where Thiassi now lived was in Jötun.
heim, a land inhabited by giants. This region was sepa.
rated from Midgard by the great river, Ocean, and lay
between Asgard and the lower world. After the gods
pronounced in favor of the dwarfs, Thiassi came here
and shut himself up in a grim stone castle, where he
spent most of his time making weapons to be used
against his foes. His dwelling was near the sea, and
rose like a jagged mountain amid the gray rocks of the
coast. A few stunted trees and bushes clung to
crevices in the rocks, and in the valleys were scanty
patches of coarse grass. A dull twilight reigned
always, and over all hung a leaden sky.

Loki's flight was very rapid, and it did not take him
long to reach Jotunheim, although it was so far from
Asgard. As he neared the coast, he made large circles,
flying far out to sea. There he saw Thiassi fishing—
a most fortunate thing; for had he been at home, it
would have been hard for Loki to reach Iduna without
his knowledge.

Next he circled around the castle, coming nearer each
time, and examining it carefully on every side. As he

passed by one of the rude openings that served as windows, a gleam like sunshine shot out into the gray twilight. Loki alighted on the edge and looked in. There, on a rough couch, lay Iduna, sleeping. There were tears on her cheeks, and the basket of golden apples was clasped firmly to her breast. Her long yellow hair filled the bare room with radiance, and the light streamed out through the opening, making a little sunshine in that land of gloom. In her sleep she sobbed, and Loki caught the word "Asgard."

Losing no time, he flew into the room, and taking his proper shape, gently awakened her. She stared vacantly for a moment, and then fear and reproach pictured themselves upon her face. "False Loki," she cried, "why are you here? Through you I am a prisoner far from Asgard!"

"Do not waste time in reproaches, fair Iduna," said Loki; "I alone can save you; and I will, if you do as I bid you." Seeing the look of distrust still on Iduna's face, he added: "You may trust me; for if I do not carry you safely back to Asgard, I am to be put to death with dreadful tortures. All the gods are growing old, and Asgard is desolate. You may thank me, after all; they will think more of you than ever when you go back with your precious fruit."

So Iduna's fears were quieted; and as there was no other hope of escape, she decided to trust herself to Loki.

"Now," said he, "grasp your basket firmly, while I say some runes that will make you as small as a nut. In that way, I can carry you safely home." Iduna did as Loki bade her, although she trembled as she felt herself growing smaller and smaller. Loki again put on his falcon plumage, and in an instant was flying towards the south. He felt quite sure that Thiassi had not seen him.

He flew more swiftly than the hawk that seeks his prey, or than the eagle that returns to her young. From time to time he turned his head to see if Thiassi, in his eagle plumage, were following him. He had gone so far that the huge castle could hardly be seen on the horizon, when above it appeared a small black speck. It was Thiassi.

The race now began in earnest. Both flew steadily for hours, high up among the leaden clouds of the cheerless sky. Loki put forth his godlike strength, and Thiassi his giant force. At last the glittering towers of Asgard gleamed against the southern sky. Would Loki reach it in time?

In the city of the gods all was expectancy from the time Loki set forth. Wily and skilful they knew him to be, but Thiassi was fierce and powerful. The result was doubtful. The gods gathered near the wall of Asgard that looked toward Jotunheim. Odin, only, sat apart, far up in his High Seat. In the dim distance he could see the mountains and castles of Jötunheim. Cold winds blew, and Asgard looked cheerless in the waning light of the afternoon. Beautiful as ever rose the stately homes of the gods; but the plains of Ida lay brown and bare, except for a few scattered snow-flakes. No summer sounds were in the air; for the birds had flown, and even the song of the cricket was hushed.

Odin kept his eyes fixed upon the distant mountains, that he might catch the first glimpse of the returning Loki. He knew, better than any one else, the vast importance of Loki's errand; and his face, grown old, and lined with care, expressed the great anxiety he felt. His ravens had not come back from their daily journey, but the two wolves lay at his feet, watching his countenance with eager eyes: near him stood Hermod, the messenger god.

Suddenly a gleam shot across the stern face of the Allfather, and a light like the fire of battle shone in his eyes. "Go, Hermod!" he cried; "tell the Æsir, Loki comes! But stay," he added: and then in a moment, "say Thiassi, clad in his eagle plumage, pursues him! The gods will soon see them from the wall of Asgard."

Hermod hastened to tell the gods, and more eagerly than ever did they scan the northern horizon for the wished-for sight.

Hermod went back to Odin, but soon rejoined the

gods, saying: "The Allfather gave Loki important in-
structions before he left Asgard. He bade him lower
his flight as he neared the city, for the mists of the
rushing river cannot harm him; but should Thiassi fly
low enough, they will burst into flames, since he is now
an enemy to the Æsir."

In a moment two specks could be seen in the north.
Then what suspense was felt by the gods! Every eye
was fixed upon the swiftly advancing birds. The Æsir
showed signs of weakness, as they stood there, and
looked older by years than when Iduna left them.
The chill wind whistled through their garments; but
they did not feel it. Nor did they see the sun as he
sank wearily behind the dark clouds in the west, as
though he too had grown old. One thought alone filled
all their minds, — "Could Loki hold out? Would he
reach Asgard before the powerful Thiassi, who seemed
to be gaining upon him?"

Nearer and nearer comes Loki. His flight is very
swift; and although the eagle is gaining upon him, the
distance is short. Will he remember to lower his flight?
Yes; he suddenly swoops down as he nears the dark
river. The gods stand breathless, with outstretched
arms. Thiassi, too, lowers his flight, forgetting the
dangerous mists. At last Loki is over the river and
over the wall, and now he falls exhausted to the ground.
But the gods heed him not, so intently are they watch-

ing Thiassi. As the eagle flies over the river, the mists burst into fierce flames, burning his wings; but he can neither stop nor turn back, his headway is so great. His scorched wings bear him over the wall, and he falls dead in their midst.

As the gods turn to look at Loki, they behold him in his natural form, and near him stands Iduna, radiant with joy, holding out with her old gracious smile her basket of golden apples. The sun, as though suddenly grown young, sends a parting stream of radiance from the west; the clouds are turned to gold; Gladsheim glitters in the distance. Youth and summer have come back to the home of the gods.

THOR AND THRYM.

Thor and Loki went to Jötunheim, in search of adventures.   On the way home, night overtook them,
and they lay down and slept on the edge of a forest.
When Thor awoke, he felt for his hammer, and it was
gone.   His wrath was terrible.   His fiery eyes and
beard darted forth lightnings, and he struck his forehead as though he would awaken from a dream.

"Loki! Loki!" he cried, "awake! Hear what I
tell you! No one on earth or in heaven knows this!
The Æsir's hammer is stolen!"

Loki's face showed surprise and bewilderment.
"Stolen!" he replied; "your hammer?   That cannot
be!"

Then they looked all about them in the grass; but
no hammer could be found.

"Thor," said Loki, "if I had Freyia's feather garment, I might find out where the hammer is. Do
you think she would lend it to me?"

"The hammer must be found," said Thor; "if not,
the giants of Jotunheim may prevail against us.
Freyia will not refuse to help me."

Very early in the morning they entered the city and

went to Freyia's palace. Many warriors feasted there each day, — mortals who had died on the field of battle, and lovers who had been faithful unto death. As they entered the wide hall, Freyia rose to greet them. And seeing that Thor's brow was dark, she said, "What ails you, Asa-Thor? Some trouble is surely in your heart!"

And Thor answered, "The hammer, Miollnir, is stolen; it is in the hands of our enemies!"

"Miollnir stolen!" cried Freyia. "How can that be? Who could take the hammer from mighty Thor?"

"I slept," said Thor, "and when I awoke, the hammer was gone. I can tell you no more."

Freyia knew well what this meant. She pondered a moment, and then said, "How can I help you, Thor?"

"Will you lend me your feather garment?" said Thor. "With the help of that, the hammer may be found."

"I would give it to you if it were made of gold, and trust it to you if it were of silver," replied Freyia.

Thor and Loki left Freyia's palace, taking with them the feather garment. When they had gone a little way, they stopped, and Loki put on the plumage and flew towards Jotunheim. He flew so swiftly that the plumage rattled.

When he reached the icy land, he saw Thrym, the Thursar's lord, sitting on a mound, plaiting gold bands for his greyhounds, and smoothing his horses' manes.

He knew Loki in spite of his disguise, and said, " How are the Æsir getting on ? And the elves ? Why have you come alone to Jótunheim?"

"The Æsir are in a bad plight ; and so are the elves," Loki replied. "Where have you hidden Thor's hammer?"

Thrym laughed aloud, and said, "I have hidden Thor's hammer eight miles beneath the earth ; and no man shall get it again unless he brings me Freyia for my wife."

When Loki heard this, he too laughed; for he was not sorry that Thor had lost his hammer.

He flew back to Asgard in the rattling plumage.

When he came near to Thor's palace, the latter saw him, and called out, " Have you had success as well as labor ? Tell me your story from the air. The man who sits down leaves out too much ; and he who lies down speaks falsely."

Loki answered from the air : " I have had labor and success. Thrym, the Thursar's lord, has your hammer. And no man can get it again unless he bring him Freyia for his wife." Then Loki flew to the ground and took off the feather garment; and he and Thor went to Freyia's palace.

When Freyia saw them, she welcomed them. Glad was she to get her falcon plumage again. But Thor's brow was dark, and he said, "Put on your bridal garments, Freyia; for we two must drive to Jotun heim."

Freyia did not understand him. So he told her that unless she became the wife of the giant Thrym, Miöll nir would never be returned.

"Make ready, therefore, and come with me!" said Thor, "or the giants will storm Asgard; and without the hammer, who can defend it against them?"

Freyia grew very angry as Thor talked. She was a mighty goddess, tall and powerful. And as her anger raged, the hall where they were trembled, and the great Brisinga[1] necklace shivered into pieces. "Never will I drive with you to Jotunheim!" cried Freyia. "Never will I be the bride of Thrym!"

Thor and Loki left the palace, and sought Odin, the wise Allfather. As soon as Odin heard what had happened, he called a council of all the gods and goddesses; for the safety of Asgard depended upon their getting back Thor's hammer.

The council met. When many had spoken to no purpose, Heimdall arose. He had the wisdom of the Vanir.

"I think I know how we may get back the hammer," he said. "Let Thor be clothed in Freyia's garments; let keys jingle at his side; place precious stones on his breast; around his neck put the famed Brisinga necklace; and set a neat coif[2] on his head. Clad thus, he

____

[1] A famous necklace made by the dwarfs.   [2] A kind of cap.

may deceive the giant, and get again the mighty hammer, Miollnir."

These words did not please Thor. He said, "The Æsir will call me womanish if I let myself be clad in bridal raiment."

Loki rejoiced secretly at the thought of Thor in woman's robes, and he said, "Speak not such words, Thor! The giants will soon rule in Asgard if you do not get back Miollnir."

The Æsir all agreed that Heimdall's words were wise. And after much urging, Thor allowed them to clothe him in Freyia's garments. They put the famed Brisinga necklace around his neck; keys jingled at his side; precious stones sparkled upon his breast; and on his head was a neat coif.

Loki was delighted, and he said to Thor, "I will go as your serving-maid; we two will drive to Jotunheim together."

The goats were found in their rocky pastures. They were quickly driven home, and hurried into the traces; and Thor and Loki leaped into the chariot. Like mountain winds let loose the goats sped on. The rocks were shivered, and the earth was in a blaze; for the mighty thunder-god drove in his wrath to Jotunheim.

When Thrym, the Thursar's lord, saw them coming, he was glad; for he thought the desire of his heart was won, — Freyia was to be his wife.

"Rise up, Jotuns!" he cried, "and deck the benches; for they bring Freyia, Niörd's daughter, from Noatun, to be my wife. Bring hither gold-horned cows and all-black oxen for the joy of the Jotuns. I had many necklaces and many treasures; but Freyia I lacked. With her I shall want nothing."

Early in the evening, many giants came to the wedding feast; and much beer was brought out for them. Thor alone devoured an ox and eight salmon, and all the sweetmeats women like. He also drank three barrels of mead.

Thrym, the king of the giants, was astonished to see a woman eat so much; and he said, "Did you ever see such a hungry bride? I never saw a bride eat so much, nor a maiden drink so much mead!"

The crafty serving-maid sat close by, and she found a ready answer. She said to the Jotun, "For eight days Freyia has eaten nothing, she has longed so for Jotunheim."

Then the giant stooped to kiss the bride under her veil; but he suddenly sprang back, saying, "Why are Freyia's looks so piercing? Methinks fire comes from her eyes."

The crafty serving-maid found again fitting words, "Well may her eyes be piercing; Freyia did not sleep for eight nights, so eager was she for Jötunheim."

The sister of the giant then came in. She, luckless woman, dared ask for a bride-gift. "Give me the ruddy rings from your hands," she said, "if you would gain my friendship and my love."

Thrym, the Thursar's lord, then said: "Bring in the hammer to consecrate the bride. Lay Miöllnir on the maiden's knees. Unite us with each other in the name of Var."[1]

When he saw the hammer, Thor's heart leaped within him. Fierce joy filled his soul at the sight of Miöllnir. He rose in his might and slew Thrym, the Thursar's lord, and crushed all the race of giants. Last of all he slew the giant's aged sister. For a bridal gift she got the stroke of Miöllnir, — blows of the hammer instead of many rings.

Thus did Odin's son get back his mighty hammer.

[1] Var or Vor, the goddess of betrothals and marriages.

THOR AND SKRYMIR.

Thor sat in his great palace, of which Odin said, "Five hundred floors, and forty eke,[1] I think, has Bilskirnir,[2] with its windings. Of all the roofed houses that I know, is my son's the greatest." The thunder-god was uneasy; for his fierce, restless spirit could never be satisfied unless warring against the giants or seeking adventures in some distant land. He went from one hall to another, and at last, with a sigh, threw himself upon a couch that was covered with the skin of a wild beast. His powerful frame showed the muscles of an athlete, and his red beard gleamed like fire.

The walls of the hall where he lay were thickly hung with shields of rare workmanship, and between them were spears and swords that flashed in the sunlight. But the glories of his great palace had no charm for Thor now; he yawned, and cast wistful glances towards the north, as though he could discern even at that distance the dreary mountains of his foes.

Suddenly a form darkened the doorway, and Loki stood before him. The thunder-god did not like Loki; he distrusted him. The love of adventure was so

---

[1] Also.   [2] "A moment-shining," so named from the lightning.

strong in both, however, that it sometimes drew them together.

"Thor," said Loki, as he entered, "order your chariot, and let us drive to Jötunheim. Asgard may do for Baldur, but I am tired of it; I long for something new."

Fire flashed from Thor's listless eyes; and he sprang up, saying, "Well spoken, Loki! Get ready; we will go at once."

They started off towards the north in Thor's heavy, rumbling chariot, drawn by the famous goats. Thor had with him three things that he never meant to leave behind: the hammer, Miollnir, which always returned to him when he flung it, and never missed the mark; the iron gloves which enabled him to grasp the hammer more firmly; and the belt of power.

They journeyed all day over barren fields and plains, and as night fell, found themselves in an almost uninhabited country. A tiny house standing on the edge of a forest was the only dwelling in sight. As they came near, some heads appeared at the doorway and suddenly disappeared. Evidently the inmates were frightened: and well they might be; for the rumbling of Thor's iron chariot sounded like thunder, and his red beard and fiery eyes flashed so in the gathering darkness that they might have been mistaken for lightning.

Thor was about to drive on, not heeding the ·house, when Loki cried imploringly: "Do stop, I pray you,

Thor! With your great strength you forget that ordinary gods may get tired and hungry after rattling about in your chariot all day with nothing to eat!"

Thor laughed heartily, and said: "I forgot who was with me; Loki and food may not long be parted. This is a small house, but it may give us food and shelter."

They alighted from the chariot and went in. The peasants cowered in one corner of the room, on seeing the wonderful strangers, so tall that they could not stand upright in the small house.

Loki spoke: "Do not be frightened, good people. We are hungry travellers who desire rest and food. We will not harm you, but will reward you generously for your hospitality."

Reassured by Loki's mild words, and Thor's good-natured smile, they came forward, still trembling. The woman made a deep courtesy, and said: "My good lords, we welcome you, and would gladly give you some supper; but the little food we had is eaten, and there is nothing left in the house; we are very poor."

"Never mind," said Thor; "do as I bid you, and I will manage the rest." Then, turning to the man, he said, "Go and unharness my goats, while your wife makes the fire and gets the pot ready; we will cook some meat."

The peasants did as Thor bade them, though they could not imagine where the meat was coming from.

Loki helped the woman make the fire, while Thor followed the man out. As soon as the goats were unharnessed, he knocked them both on the head with his hammer, and told the peasant to prepare them for cooking. Soon an enormous platter of goats' flesh was smoking on the table.

As Thor helped the peasants and their two children to the meat, he said : "Eat all you will, good people, but beware of breaking the bones. I have a special reason for wishing them to be kept whole."

Thialfi, the son, had rarely tasted meat, so this was a great feast for him. As he was picking the meat from one of the thigh-bones, Loki whispered, "The marrow inside the bone is best of all!" and Thialfi, forgetting Thor's command, cracked the bone and sucked out the marrow.

Raska, his sister, ate but little. She spent her time in gazing with open-mouthed wonder at the tall strangers who ate with such evident relish the goats that served them as horses. And she asked herself what they would do on the morrow, with the heavy iron chariot, and no goats to draw it.

After the hearty meal all were soon fast asleep.

Thor awoke as the first rays of the early dawn shot into the little room. Jumping up quickly, he gathered together the bones of the goats and put them into the skins. Then lifting his mighty hammer, he repeated some magic words, called runes. Instantly the two goats were skipping about as lively as if they had enjoyed a good meal and a night's rest instead of having served as food for others; but Thor noticed that one of them limped. Suspecting the cause, he became furious with anger, and called out in a loud voice, "Wake up, you wretched peasants! See what you have done to my goats!"

The peasants started as though waked by a thunderclap, and cowered, trembling, before the angry god.

"Who broke the thigh-bone of my goat?" roared Thor, clutching Miöllner till his knuckles grew white, while flashes of light came from his eyes and beard, threatening to burn the room.

Then Thialfi, who was a brave lad, plucked up his courage, and said: "Oh! mighty sir, I broke the thigh-bone of your goat. I forgot what you said; the meat was so good; and I wanted to get the marrow. Punish me, but do not harm the others; they have done nothing."

The boy's courage and honesty touched Thor, who was really kind at heart. And he said: "You have done a very bad deed; but I will forgive you, because you are brave and speak the truth. A liar and a coward I cannot abide. But you are too good a fellow to spend your life in this hut like a beast. Come with me, and you shall see the world. Your sister shall come.

too. You shall live in a big house. If this little hut were put into it, you might hunt all day and not find it."

Then Thor gave the peasant and his wife a handful of gold, saying, "Your children shall come and see you when they will." And when they were starting off, he said, "I leave the goats and the chariot in your care until my return. Do not break any bones!"—and he laughed heartily.

So the four started into the thick forest. Thialfi, who was very fleet of foot, carried the bag containing food for the journey; and Raska, who was a stout peasant-girl, kept up easily with the others. After a long walk through the forest, they came to the great river, Ocean, on the other side of which lay Jótunheim. They crossed the sea without much trouble, although it was a long distance over it.

On the other side was a land much wilder than the one they left behind. Everything was enormous in size; the stones being as large as rocks, and the trees reaching to the clouds. After crossing a barren stretch of country, strewn with huge bowlders, they came to a deep forest where perfect silence reigned, and where there was nothing green under foot, for the ground was covered with pine-needles. It was like twilight in this forest even at noon; the thick branches let so little sunlight through; and besides, the sun never shone brightly in any part of Jotunheim.

All day they travelled on, and one part of the wood was so exactly like another that they might have gone about in a circle had not Thialfi now and then climbed to the top of a tall tree to make sure that they were going in the right direction.

As night fell, the little light that filtered through the branches faded away, leaving them in utter darkness. It was impossible to go on without running against the trees. Thor, impatient as he was to proceed, decided to stop and wait for the morning. In the darkness they felt around for a good place to sleep. As Loki was groping about, he touched something that was not a tree; and, as he ran his hand up, it seemed like the entrance to a house.

"This is very strange!" he exclaimed. "Strike a light, Thialfi! here is some kind of a house, but whoever lives in it must be fond of the woods!"

Thialfi did as Loki requested, and by the flaring light of a dry stick they could distinguish a large opening. A dwelling of some kind it was, certainly, but of a new pattern; for the door was the size of the whole front of the house.

"There's nothing like travelling to see strange sights!" said Loki. And as they went in, he remarked, "This house is of an odd shape, but it seems to be a good place to sleep in."

They threw themselves down on the floor of the large entrance hall, and were soon fast asleep.

About midnight they were awakened by a terrible shaking of the earth, together with a rumbling noise like thunder. They started up, expecting to feel another shock in a moment, for apparently it was an earthquake. But all was still. Thor placed himself in the main door of the house, while the others found some smaller rooms that promised greater quiet.

As soon as the first rays of the sun struggled through the branches, so that Thor could distinguish one object from another, he fastened on his belt of strength, drew on his iron gauntlets, and grasping his hammer firmly, strode out into the forest to seek the cause of the noise and the shaking that had so disturbed their slumbers. He expected to find a mighty chasm yawning near by, — the result of the earthquake.

He had not gone far, when he saw a hill rising in an opening amid the trees ; and at the same time he heard a loud sound that evidently came from the further side of the hill. When Thor reached that side, he could just distinguish in the dim light, the enormous head of a giant from whose open mouth came the sounds he had heard. What Thor had taken for a hill was the giant's body. His eyes were closed, and his eye-brows stood out like lines of bushes from above them. His hair looked more like a forest of trees than like the hair of a common person.

Thor looked at the sleeping giant for a moment and then aimed his hammer at his forehead. But instead of flinging it, he stopped short, and reaching up, put his mouth near his ear, and roared in a voice of thunder, "What is your name?"

The giant stretched his huge limbs, and slowly opened his eyes. At first he seemed dazed; but gradually a look of intelligence came into his face, and he said, slowly, " Did anybody speak ?"

"Yes," roared Thor, "I did. What's your name?"

As the giant heard Thor's voice, he turned his large head slowly around and looked at him. After a long stare, he replied, "Skrymir." Then he added, "I know you; you are Asa-Thor."

"You had better thank me," said Thor ; "I seldom begin my acquaintance with giants in so polite a manner, as some of your friends have learned to their cost."

Skrymir smiled, but it took a good while. After another pause he broke the silence with, " What have you done with my glove ?" And he slowly stretched out his hand and picked up the house where they had spent the night. Luckily Loki and the others had just left it. There was a look of amusement on Skrymir's enormous features that irritated Thor greatly ; but he tried to look unconcerned.

At last the giant got up, shook his huge limbs, and said, good-naturedly: "Will you little people accept of the company of such a large person as myself? I should like to join you; and we may be useful to one another, although we differ in size."

Thor accepted Skrymir's offer, but his words angered him so that he clutched Miollnir. The giant next untied an immense provision sack in which he carried his food, and began to eat his breakfast. Thor, who could enjoy the society of giants only when he was fighting them, went off to a little distance and ate with his companions.

As they were finishing their meal, the giant came crashing through the woods to where they were, and said: "Here, friends, I am big, and you are small. Put your provisions into my sack. I can carry everything easily."

There was no reason for refusing the offer of the good-natured giant, so they put all the food into his sack. He flung the bag over his shoulder, and led the way with long strides.

It was a hard day's journey. But Thor was too proud to own that they could not easily keep up with a giant; so instead of asking him to slacken his pace, they ran all the way.

Toward night, Skrymir stopped under a large oak. Flinging himself down, he handed the provision sack to Thor, saying, "Here, Asa-Thor, take this. I am more sleepy than hungry, and do not care for food." In an instant he was sound asleep, and snoring so loudly that the woods resounded and the earth trembled.

Thor took the bag and started to untie the strings; but with all his efforts not a knot would come undone, nor could he even loosen one. At this his blood began to boil; and seizing Miollnir, he flung it with all his might at the head of the sleeping giant.

Skrymir stirred a little, put his hand to his head, and slowly opened his large blue eyes, saying, "Did a leaf fall on my head? I thought I felt something." Then looking at Thor, he asked, "Have you eaten your supper yet? Aren't you going to bed?"

"Yes," replied Thor; "we are going to bed." And as he would not ask Skrymir to untie the sack, they lay down, hungry and tired, under a tree, not very far from the giant.

Skrymir made such a roaring that it was almost impossible to sleep. As Thor lay there, hearing the dreadful noise, he grew more and more furious. At last he started up with an oath, and going to where the giant lay, swung Miöllnir with all his Asa-might, and plunged it into his forehead up to the handle.

The giant stopped snoring, and turning uneasily, muttered, "What is the matter now? Did an acorn fall upon my forehead? Where are you, Thor?"

Then, with a sigh, he was fast asleep again, and snoring as loudly as ever.

Thor was by this time so angry that, even had all been quiet, he could not have slept. He sat for hours leaning against the tree, his comrades asleep near him. Instead of growing calmer, he grew more enraged as the hours went by.

When the morning light showed again the outlines of the giant's huge form, he went over to where he lay. This time he swung Miollnir as he had never swung it before, and buried it so deeply in the giant's temple that only a little of the handle stuck out. "Can you feel that?" he roared.

Skrymir opened his eyes, and as they rested upon the angry god, asked sleepily: "Are there any birds on the tree above me? I thought some moss fell upon my forehead." Then opening his eyes wider, he added, "But it is morning, and we must start on."

When they were ready to go, the giant turned to Thor with an odd smile on his face, and said, "You evidently think me rather large, Asa-Thor; but when you reach Utgard, you will find larger men than I. Let me give you some advice: do not brag too much. Utgard-Loki, the lord of Utgard, and his big courtiers will not stand the boasting of little men like you. In fact, the best thing you can do is to turn back and give up visiting Utgard. Dangers that you little suspect may lie before you in that giant-land."

Thor tried to answer Skrymir, but he was so choked with rage that the words would not come out.

The giant continued, "If you are determined to go on, turn to the east, toward the mountains that you see yonder." And taking the provision sack, he disappeared in the woods.

Thor started after him with Miollnir; but he seemed to have changed suddenly into a large gray mountain at their right.

As the giant had carried off the food, they were forced to content themselves with the few berries and roots that they could find on their way; for there was no game in the woods.

About noon the forest ended abruptly, and they came into a large plain that extended on all sides like a gray sea. There were rocks here and there; but not a blade of grass, not a tree gladdened the eye as it roamed over the dreary waste. In the midst of the plain was a huge castle. Even at that distance they had to bend back their necks in order to see its turrets, half hidden by clouds. It looked as though carved roughly by giants out of a rocky mountain. Its rude walls bore the scars of time, and showed in places the fierce sport of the lightning.

Thor and his companions went towards the castle,

clambering over the bowlders. It was farther off than they had thought: its great size made it seem near. When at last they stood before the high walls that surrounded it, night was beginning to fall. The great god Thor seemed but a child as he stretched up his hand to reach the lock of the ponderous gate. In vain; it was too high for him. Loki had already wriggled between the bars; and he now called to the others to follow him. Once inside the walls, they saw through the open door of the castle a hall larger than Thor's whole palace.

The gods and their companions walked in boldly and looked about. They could see clouds floating in and out through jagged openings in the vast heights above. In the centre of the hall was a table of rough granite which was supported by monsters whose wide-open jaws made huge caverns. At the upper end of the table was Utgard-Loki, the giant-king. He sat on a high seat, the back and arms of which were formed by the coils of the Midgard serpent sculptured in stone. The huge, horrid head of the monster stretched out over the king. The beard of Utgard-Loki was the color of the gray rocks, and fell in masses to the ground. His motions were heavy and slow. When he reached his hand for the beer-mug which stood near him on the table, it was some time before it reached his lips; and after a long drink he would give a sigh of satisfaction that sounded like the roaring of the wind. His features were slow in changing their expression. His large round eyes were neither kind nor fierce; for they had no more human feeling in them than cold mountain lakes.

On each side of the table there were stone benches whose high backs made comfortable resting-places for the heads of the giants. These giants were nearly as large as Utgard-Loki, and all were drinking beer. Some one had evidently made a joke just before Thor and his companions entered; for a deep, slow, "Ha! ha!" came from one and then another of the giants, until the roar of their great guffaws filled the vast hall, and rolled out like thunder into the gathering night. The gods could examine everything at their leisure; for not one of the giants seemed aware of their presence.

Thor's blood began to boil as he looked at the dull, mountain-like creatures; and he longed to fling his hammer and change them into real mountains as they sat on their benches of stone; but he forebore, and going up to Utgard-Loki, placed himself directly in front of him. The king turned his expressionless eyes upon him, and after staring for several moments, burst into a loud laugh, showing his granite teeth.

"Why, what have I before me?" he roared. "This stripling must be Asa-Thor of whom I have often heard.

I am surprised! but perhaps you are really bigger than you look!" Then in a moment he added: "What can you do? We always make our guests prove their strength or their skill before we invite them to eat and drink with us."

Loki was very hungry, and pushing himself in front of Thor, he cried eagerly, "I will wager that no one here can eat as fast as I can!" And he laughed to himself at the thought of contending with the slow, clumsy giants.

Then Utgard beckoned to a man that Loki had not noticed. He sat at the lower end of the table, and was small and agile compared with the giants. A trough full of meat was brought in.

"Logi," said the king, "show this little man that giants can be as quick as he."

They began to eat, seated at opposite ends of the trough. Loki ate ravenously; for pride and hunger both spurred him on. Neither stopped to look at the other, till at last they met in the very middle of the trough. Loki then saw, to his amazement, that while he had eaten all the meat on his side, Logi had consumed, not only the meat, but the bones, and even the trough itself. So there was no question as to who had won the victory. However, the fact that he had enjoyed a hearty meal consoled Loki in part for his defeat.

Utgard next turned his eyes to where Thialfi stood ;

and pointing at him with his huge forefinger, asked, "What can that young man do?"

Thialfi straightened up, and answered proudly: "I can run a race with any one you may appoint. He must be swifter than the eagle if he can outrun me!"

The king rose slowly from his seat and walked with a lumbering gait through the vast hall and out upon the plain surrounding the castle. A few giants followed, one after another, and seated themselves on the large bowlders that lay around.

Utgard-Loki pointed out the course, and then called in a loud voice, "Hugi, come here!"

Quick as a flash appeared an agile little fellow, apparently more akin to the elves than to the giants. A peculiar, dull smile overspread the features of the king as he said, "We do not match you little people against our giants; that would be hardly fair; this is one of our dwarfs." And he and his courtiers laughed loud and long at the joke.

The course pointed out was a long one, but Thialfi started like a steed of high mettle eager for the race. He flew as the swallow flies. Yet Hugi was so much swifter, that he touched the goal and met Thialfi on the return before the latter had finished the course.

Utgard-Loki laughed, saying, "You must ply your legs better, little Thialfi; though you are a very fair runner!"

They ran a second time; and when Hugi turned back from the goal, Thialfi was a good bow-shot from it.

"Well run, Thialfi!" cried the king of the giants; "no better runner has ever visited us ; but, for once, you have evidently found your match. One more course shall decide the contest."

This time Thialfi sped as swiftly as the winds that rush over the open plain; one could hardly see him as he flew along. Yet still his rival outstripped him; and when they met, Thialfi was not half-way to the goal. Even Thor cried out that it was enough. And eager to show that he, at least, could outdo the giants, he demanded a trial of his powers.

"Let me show your courtiers how an Asa can drink!" he said. "I do not fear to contend with the mightiest of you!"

They returned to the hall; and Utgard-Loki, again seating himself on his high throne, called out to his cup-bearer, "Bring hither our ancient drinking-horn!" Then he explained to Thor that it was from this horn that his courtiers were obliged to drink when they had trespassed in any way against the established usage of the land.

When the cup-bearer brought the horn, Thor found that while it was not very large at the top, it was exceedingly long, winding in coil after coil, so that it was hard to distinguish the end. Indeed, it reached far across the hall, and was there lost in the shadows. Thor gazed at it with interest. He saw that strange sea-monsters were carved upon it, and that its coils were encrusted with shells and barnacles, and fringed with sea-mosses.

The god was very thirsty, and with an expression of satisfaction he raised the horn to his lips. Long and deep was his draught. As he drank, the sound was like that of water breaking upon a pebbly beach. Yet when he stopped, breathless, and looked to see how much beer was left in the horn, he found, to his surprise, that there was about as much as at first.

Raising the horn again, he drank as long as he could without taking breath, and then looked in. The liquor had sunk even less than before.

Utgard-Loki smiled broadly, and said, "How now, Thor! Have you not saved for the third draught more than you can make away with? You must not spare yourself too much in a test of this kind. If you wish to drain the horn, you must drink deep!"

Thor was in a towering passion as he raised the horn for the third time. It seemed as though he would never stop drinking. The noise he made was like the roar of the waves as they dash upon the rocks in a storm; and yet, when he stopped and looked at the horn, the liquor was so high that it could only just be carried without spilling.

Shame and anger were pictured on Thor's face as he gave back the horn to the cup-bearer. "I own myself beaten," he said; "but let me try something else: I know I can outdo you giants in something."

"There is a little game our children sometimes play," said the king; "supposing you try that. I would not propose a child's game to Thor, had he not shown himself much weaker than I thought him. See if you can lift my cat from the ground."

As he was speaking, a large gray cat ran across the hall. Thor sprang towards her, and putting his hand under her body, tried to lift her from the ground; but as he raised his hand, she curved her back, and with his utmost efforts he could only raise one foot from the floor.

"Just as I expected," said Utgard-Loki; "the cat is large, and Thor is small compared with our men."

"You call me small," cried Thor, thoroughly enraged; — "but which of you dares wrestle with me now that I am angry?" and his eyes darted forth sparks, and from his beard shot flames of fire, lighting up the gray hall.

"I see no one here," said the king, looking around, "who would not think it beneath him to wrestle with a little man like you. But here comes my old nurse Elli; she has thrown to the ground many a man as strong and boastful as Thor."

An old woman, bent nearly double, came into the

hall. She was toothless, and had scant, gray locks. Her thin form trembled as she raised her bleared and almost sightless eyes to Thor. He looked at her with disgust.

"Wrestle with him, mother," said Utgard-Loki.

Whereupon she wound her long, thin arms about Thor, and the more he tried to throw her, the more firmly did she stand. At last, worn out with the conflict, the god sank upon one knee.

The king then stepped forward and said it was enough. Then he added, "Although you little people have shown yourselves weak compared with us giants, still we admire your spirit, and we invite you to eat and drink with us."

Thor and his companions were by this time thoroughly vexed and humbled. They gave up the contest, and accepted the hospitality of Utgard-Loki.

Long was the feast, and strange and dull were the stories told by the giants as they nodded over the foaming beer. Thor, as he sat in the dreary stone hall, thought of the wit and gayety that reigned in Gladsheim. But the giants seemed to be enjoying themselves.

The gods awoke at daybreak, and Utgard-Loki went with them through the iron gate. When on the other side he said: "What do you think of your journey, Asa-Thor? Do you consider that you have met your match among the giants this time?"

"I own myself beaten," said Thor; "I am ashamed. It vexes me to think in what esteem you must hold me."

"Well, Asa-Thor," replied the giant, "since you are beyond my castle walls, I will tell you the truth, if it will be any comfort to you. And first, let me say, that never again shall you or any Asa enter within my walls!

"I have all along deceived you by enchantments. It was I who met you in the forest, and there I found out how strong you were. The provision sack which you tried in vain to untie was fastened with iron; that was why you could not open it. The blows of your hammer were so mighty that the first one would have killed me had I not, by magic, brought a mountain between us. On your return you will see a mountain with three square glens, each deeper than the one before it. Those are the marks left by your hammer.

"In the same way I deceived you in your contests with my courtiers. Loki ate like hunger itself; but Logi was wild-fire, and that consumes all that is set before it. Thialfi's running struck us all with amazement, for he outstripped the wind; but Hugi was my thought, and that can fly more swiftly than the lightning as it flashes from peak to peak. When you tried to empty our ancient horn, you performed a feat so marvellous that had I not seen it myself I should never have believed it. The end of the horn, which you could not see, reached to the ocean. You drank so deeply that you lowered the great river. When you reach it on your way home, you will see how the water has fallen. In Midgard they will henceforth call this the ebb. When you lifted from the ground one paw of my cat, you were in reality raising the great Midgard serpent that encircles the earth. And you lifted him so high that you nearly pulled his tail out of his mouth. We feared the foundations of Jotunheim would be shaken. But your wrestling with Elli was the most astonishing feat of all. She was no other than old age. And there never has been, and never will be, a man whom old age cannot lay low, if he abide her coming. You are a mighty god, Asa-Thor, and I shall take good care that you never find my country again, however diligently you may seek for it. We giants, dull and heavy as we may seem, have the wisdom of the ages."

Thor raised his hammer, but Utgard-Loki had vanished. And turning his eyes to where the castle was, he saw nothing but a beautiful green plain, upon which the slow-moving clouds cast their shadows.

Thor returned to his home in Asgard; but the memory of his adventures in the castle of Utgard-Loki stung him continually; and he determined to revenge himself by attacking the Midgard serpent in his ocean home.

THOR'S JOURNEY TO GET THE KETTLE FOR ÆGIR.

ÆGIR, the ruler of the stormy western sea, feasted all the gods at harvest time ; but there was never quite enough beer to go round. This angered Thor, for it showed a lack of hospitality; and he told Ægir, very bluntly, what he thought of it.

Ægir appeared to feel hurt, and said: "Your words are rude and unkind, Asa-Thor ; the reason why the beer does not hold out is, that I have no kettle large enough for the brewing. It is no small matter to make beer for all the dwellers in Asgard."

Tyr, who stood near, turned to Thor, and said: "My father, the fierce giant Hymir, dwells near heaven's end. He owns a caldron a mile deep. I think we can manage in some way to get it from him. Ægir will then have the satisfaction of entertaining his friends in a manner befitting his generous nature."

"It is too bad to trouble you," said Ægir; "it is such a long journey, and you may not be able to get the caldron, after all."

"Oh, friend Ægir!" cried Thor, "we count nothing as trouble if it only obliges you. Come, Tyr, let us be off! My goats are ready, and I long to see Jötunheim again. If I can only meet the Midgard serpent on this journey, I will pay him well for deceiving me as he did at Utgard-Loki's — making me lift him for a cat!"

So the two gods started off together. Tyr was a more fit companion for Thor than Loki was. He was as fearless as the thunder-god himself, and one of the noblest of the Æsir.

Thor put up his goats at some distance from the giant's castle; for wherever he went in his great rumbling chariot he was known as the mighty god of thunder; and this time he wished to go quietly.

Night was coming on as they neared the dwelling of Hymir, which stood by the frozen shore, surrounded by rocks and icebergs. The sides of the huge castle glistened with frost, and from its projections hung long icicles. As they went in through the wide door, the first object to meet their eyes was a giantess with nine hundred heads. She was nodding sleepily with all her heads in a corner of the vast hall; and she did not notice them. This was Hymir's mother.

A great fire of pine and fir trees burned at one end of the room, and near it sat a lovely woman, the fire-light shining on her golden-brown hair. She greeted her son and his friend joyfully, and brought beer to refresh them after their long journey. Then looking out into the night, she said: "My husband will soon be nome from his fishing. But he is often in an ill-humor, and the sight of guests might put him in a rage. Fearless as you are, do as I bid you; hide under those kettles at the other end of the room. It is dark there, and he will not see you." They did as she bade them.

Before long there was a loud rushing and roaring sound; it was Hymir coming home from his fishing, wading through the sea. Great waves broke upon the rocks and icebergs; and the sound of the giant's breathing was like the roaring of winds. The earth trembled beneath his tread, and the walls of the castle were shaken. As he entered, the gods saw that his huge head glistened with ice and snow and that "the thicket on his cheeks was frozen." With a grunt of ill-humor he threw down his net in which were whales and other sea-monsters, not yet dead.

His wife rose up, trembling, to meet him, and spoke gently, saying: "You must be tired, my husband, after your hard day's fishing. You see I have a good fire, and supper will soon be ready. It is a fierce night. Even you must have found it hard coming through the sea." A rough growl was the only reply to her kind words.

After Hymir had sat by the fire some time, and had taken great draughts of hot beer, his wife spoke to him again, saying: "I have been thinking much of our son Tyr of late; and, strange to say, he came home to-day;

and he brought his friend Thor with him, — Thor, the great thunder-god. I know you will be glad to see them."

"Where are they?" roared Hymir; and he glanced toward the dark end of the hall, where the kettles hung. The huge wooden beam broke as his eyes rested upon it, and eight kettles fell, all breaking but one. That one was the largest of all, a hard hammered caldron. The gods then stood forth, their shapely forms in strange contrast with the huge, uncouth figure of the giant. When Hymir saw the flashing of Thor's eyes, he felt that it boded evil to him.

Three oxen were cooked for supper, and Thor ate two of them. The giant, thinking such a guest would soon make havoc in his larder, said gruffly, "We shall have to live on what we can catch in the sea, to-morrow!"

"Nothing would suit me better than to go fishing with you, giant Hymir," said Thor.

The next morning the giant got ready for the expedition. Being in a bad humor, he said, "Get your own bait if you are going with me! You can catch an ox for yourself."

Thor found the herd of the giant, and going up to a coal-black bull, the finest of all, wrung his head from his neck and took it for bait.

When Hymir saw the head of his best bull, he said,

"I wish you had sat quiet, and had let me get the bait!"

They started out in Hymir's boat, both rowing. Thor's mighty strokes sent the boat scudding over the angry sea. When they were far out, the giant said: "This is my fishing-ground. Here I catch whales. We will stop."

"It is child's play to fish so near the shore," said Thor, redoubling the might of his strokes.

The sea grew rougher, and great waves broke over the boat. When at last they were in the very middle of the ocean, Thor stopped rowing. The giant at once threw his line, and drew up two whales with one bait.

Then Thor took out a line, which although slender was of great strength. He fastened the gory head of the black ox firmly to the hook. Down, down went the bait, far below the rough waves; deeper than where the whales sported; down to the very bottom of the ocean. There lay the mighty earth-encircler, the giant serpent of the deep.[1] For years he had lain in the quiet of the deep sea, with his tail down his throat, waiting with slow-burning hatred for the time of vengeance, the Twilight of the Gods. The coils of his mighty body were fringed with sea-mosses, and covered with clinging

[1] See Œlenschlæger's poem, "Thor's Fishing," in Longfellow's Poets and Poetry of Europe. The same poem may be found in Frye's transla-tion of Œlenschlæger's "Gods of the North."

shells. Tall sea-palms waved gently in the dim waters above his head. Never, in all the long years, had bait with hook come near his dull eyes.

Thor had secured a most tempting bait. The gory head of the ox came near the serpent's head, and then floated slowly away like a living thing. Then it came near again. A look of eagerness came into the serpent's cruel eyes, and he drew his tail slowly from his jaws. As it reached him the third time, he opened wide his jaws, snatched it, and swallowed head, hook, and all. Then came the struggle.

Thor pulled with such strength that his feet broke through the bottom of the boat, and he stood on the floor of the sea. The serpent, hissing and lashing with pain, was drawn up through the vast depths of mid-ocean. The sea, away to the horizon, was covered with poisonous foam. High waves rose like tossing mountains over the vast expanse. Heavy clouds met the waters, and Thor's lightnings darted amid the seething billows. The horrid coils of the great serpent rose above the sea, glistening with venom, and his huge jaws gaped as he strove to seize his powerful enemy.

Thor grasped him in his arms, and the struggle grew fiercer still. Sheets of poisonous foam mixed with the clouds. The crashing of the thunder mingled with the loud hissing of the serpent ; and except for the lightning, darkness covered the sea. Thor loosed his hold

of the monster for an instant that he might hurl Miöllnir at his head. Then the giant, who saw with fear and
hatred the triumph of the god, cut the line; and with a
long hiss of vengeful hate, the serpent sank back into
the sea; there to await Ragnarok, the Twilight of the
Gods.

Thor's rage and disappointment knew no bounds.
He struck the giant a blow that sent him reeling from
his boat into the boiling sea. Then he himself started
on foot through the ocean, carrying the boat, and all it
contained. But Hymir recovered, and reached the
shore soon after Thor.

They supped upon the two whales that the giant had
caught. As soon as they had finished eating, Thor
asked for the famous kettle, Mile-deep, hinting that
Hymir might fear the consequences should he refuse
to give it to him.

"Asa-Thor," said the giant, "you are asking a great
favor, and you should give me one more proof of your
strength before expecting me to do so much for you."
Rising from his seat he took from a shelf a huge drink-
ing-cup, and handing it to Thor, said, "If you can
break this cup, you shall have the kettle!"

Thor first threw the cup at an upright stone that
served as a seat. The stone broke in two, but the cup
remained whole. Then, with all his might, he flung it
at one of the pillars of the hall. The column was

shattered, but the cup was unhurt, showing not even a dent.

Then Tyr's mother whispered in Thor's ear, "Strike at the head of Hymir; that is harder than any cup."

Tightening his belt of strength, Thor again threw the cup, and this time full at Hymir's forehead. The cup was shattered to atoms.

Then was Hymir astounded and troubled. "That was a good cup," he said; "never again can I say, when the beer is handed to me, 'Beer, thou art too hot.'" And thinking it best to be rid of so dangerous a guest as soon as possible, he said to Thor, "Now 'tis to be seen whether you can carry Mile-deep out of our dwelling."

Tyr went up to the huge iron pot, and tried to lift it; but he could only tip it a little toward one side. Then Thor, with his iron gloves, grasped it by the brim, while his feet burst through the floor; and putting it upon his head, he started off, the rings jingling about his heels. Tyr followed him.

They had not gone far when they heard a loud noise behind them; and turning around they saw a mighty band of frost giants, with Hymir at their head. Some brandished great stone clubs, while others carried bowlders and blocks of ice to throw at the Æsir; they shouted and roared as they came on. Then Thor put down Mile-deep, and grasping Miöllnir, hurled it at

the savage crew. Instantly all was still; and in place
of the noisy giants, a line of snowy mountains raised
their heads to the sky.

Thor and Tyr soon reached the place where the
goats were tied, and putting the kettle into the chariot,
drove rapidly toward Ægir's halls. They were delayed
a little because the goat whose thigh-bone had been
injured fell down, and then went lame. But in spite
of this, they were not long in reaching Ægir's palace.
The sea-god welcomed them, but looked with dismay
at Mile-deep, knowing how great a brewing there would
have to be in the future, when he feasted the gods.

FREY[1] CLIMBS INTO ODIN'S HIGH SEAT.

FREY was the ruler of the light-elves. He therefore spent the greater part of his time in Alfheim, the home of the elves, in the lower world. He was often in Asgard, however, and his kind heart and joyous nature made him a great favorite there.

One afternoon he arrived in the city just as the sun was setting, and found it almost deserted. He wandered about for a time, feeling very forlorn. He looked at the glittering palaces whose towers reached to the clouds; and then his gaze went higher still, and rested upon Odin's High Seat, the most sacred place in Asgard. Suddenly he was seized with an intense desire to climb up and see for once all that the mighty Odin saw when he looked abroad each day. The All-father had never said that no one but himself might sit in that sacred place; but had any god ventured to climb up there, he would have been thought very presuming, if not worse. Knowing this, Frey hesitated, while his eyes rested longingly upon the gleaming point.

At last, with an air of determination, he entered the great palace from which the High Seat shot up, and

---

[1] Frey, a Van-god; ruler of the light-elves.

was soon on his way upward. He was so anxious to reach the top that he did not once stop to look around ; but with all his efforts the way seemed long. When at last he reached the top, breathless and weary, his curiosity gave him no rest. With eager eyes he looked upon the awe-inspiring scene.

Asgard lay just below, glowing with beauty in the warm western light. Below Asgard could be seen a portion of Midgard, the home of men, with the great river, Ocean, surrounding it. While towards the north, on the other side of the ocean, was the gloomy giant-land, called Jotunheim. Far below Midgard and Jotunheim stretched the great under-world. Had Frey's eyes been as keen as Odin's, he could have discerned more clearly the outlines of this vast region which stretched beyond the narrow bounds of the upper-worlds. A part of it was hidden by Midgard and Jötunheim: but Frey could see that the northern part was dark and misty, except where Heimdall's shining castle sent its rays ; while the southern portion glowed with a beautiful light. This light he knew came from the realms where Urd and her two sisters lived, guarding the sacred well, under Yggdrasil's third root. Mimir's land he could not see, except the eastern part, where lay Alfheim, his own bright home ; but in the west he could see the land of the Vanir, the great race to which he himself belonged. As he looked more closely he felt sure that he could distinguish his father's castle, Noatun, by the sea.

His curiosity was satisfied at last, and he was just turning away, when a gleam from the north, from icy Jötunheim, caught his eye. As he looked keenly in that direction, he saw a beautiful giant-maiden, lifting her fair white arms to undo the latch of a gate in the castle wall. The gleam of light that had attracted him came from her snow-white arms and her golden hair. Frey was so astonished to see such a sight in the land of cold and darkness, that he could not take his eyes away. As the maiden passed through the gate, she turned her face toward Asgard for a moment, and Frey fancied that her large blue eyes looked appealingly up to him. The keenness of Odin's sight must have been granted to him just then, or he never could have seen all this so plainly. The vision lasted but a moment. The maiden disappeared behind the castle wall, and Jötunheim lay in darkness.

It seemed to Frey that when the gleam of her snow-white arms vanished from the land of the giants, the light of day faded from all the worlds. Even Asgard was dark and gloomy. Frey's heart felt strangely heavy. Never had the merry master of the elves known sorrow. His life had been one long, bright summer day. A strange, new feeling possessed him.

With a heavy step, he went slowly down the winding

stairs. When he reached the city, it was still deserted. So he entered the spacious hall of Gladsheim and threw himself upon one of the richly carved seats. When the gods returned, he tried to assume his usual cheerfulness, but all noticed the change in him; and he was thankful when the shadows deepened and he could be alone. Sleep would not come, however. One picture was continually before his eyes, — the fair giant-maiden with her gleaming white arms and her sad blue eyes.

FREY'S LOVE FOR GERD.

SKADI was the wife of Niord,[1] Frey's father. She was the daughter of Thiassi, who was killed by the burning mists of the Asgard river. The gods were sorry for Thiassi's death, because, although he had tried to injure them, he had in the past done them great services. So, to honor his memory, Odin placed his eyes in the heavens, where they shone like stars. Then he sent for Skadi, his daughter, to come to Asgard; and soon after, she became the wife of Niord. Niord's home was in the Vanirland; but both he and Skadi were often in Asgard with the Æsir.

Skadi had grown very fond of Frey; and when she found him pale and sad on the morning after he had climbed to the High Seat, she tried in every way to comfort him, but in vain. She sent him to Iduna; but for once her golden apples were powerless. As he grew sadder and weaker, all known remedies were tried, but his malady would yield to none of them. And no one could find out the cause of his trouble.

Frey had a friend named Skirnir; a mortal he was said to be, who lived with the gods in Asgard. He

---

[1] A Van-god; father of Frey and Freyia.

was like a brother to Frey; as children they had played together, and nothing had ever come between them to mar their perfect friendship. He had given Frey a wonderful sword, — the fatal sword made by Thiassi. Skirnir was a great traveller, and in one of his journeys he visited Mimir. The latter thought that the Æsir should possess the dangerous weapon, so he gave it to Skirnir; and he, on his return to Asgard, gave it to Frey. Frey valued it above all his possessions; for it was a sword of rare beauty, and it was sure to kill the foe against whom it was used.

Skirnir was away when Frey fell sick, and when he got home, he was shocked at the change in his friend; he was so pale and sad, and so languid in his movements. Skadi told Skirnir all they had done to cure her son of his mysterious sickness; and she begged Skirnir to get from him the secret of his trouble.

Skirnir talked with him; and Frey felt so sure of the love and sympathy of his friend, that he told him everything, — how he had climbed to the High Seat, and had seen the beautiful giant-maiden, and how from that time the thought of her had not left him; for if he slept a few moments, it was only to dream of her, and to see her sad blue eyes gazing at him.

"My heart has grown so heavy," said Frey, "that I think I shall not live long unless I can have the giant-maiden for my wife. But that can never be! The

Æsir would not hear to such a thing. And even could I gain their consent, how could I get the good will of her parents, who are hostile giants? Perhaps even her own heart is cold towards me. Sometimes I think she did not see me at all as she glanced towards Asgard, and that the look I thought I saw in her eyes was not really there."

Skirnir pondered a few moments, and then said: "I think I can help you, Frey. The gods are so concerned about your health, that I am sure they will consent to the marriage, however little they may like it. And as for the maiden herself, and her parents, let me arrange with them. You know I have been on many difficult errands, and have always succeeded. Rest quietly. I will come back soon and consult with you about my journey to Jötunheim."

Skirnir left Frey, and went to Odin and the other gods to talk the matter over with them. He told them that love for the giant-maiden, Gerd, was the cause of Frey's sickness, and that in order to be cured, he must have the maiden for his wife. When the gods learned this, they agreed to sanction the marriage.

SKIRNIR'S JOURNEY TO WIN GERD FOR FREY.

SKIRNIR went quickly back to Frey and told him that the gods consented to his marriage with Gerd, the giant-maiden. When Frey heard this, the weary look left his face, and the light of hope shone in his eyes. Joy gave him strength; and he helped his friend make ready for the dangerous journey.

Two things Skirnir must have, — Odin's horse and Frey's sword. Sleipnir would carry him safely through the flames with which, no doubt, the giant surrounded his castle; and Frey's sword would protect him in fight. Iduna gave him eleven golden apples to win the heart of the maiden; and Odin, his wonderful ring made by the dwarfs.

By the time Skirnir was ready to start, night was over Asgard; and as he mounted Sleipnir, he spoke to him, saying: " Dark is it without; it is time for us to go over the misty fells, over the giant's land. We shall both return, or the powerful giant will seize us both. We will not desert one another ! " The horse turned his ears back and listened as Skirnir spoke to him. Then he sped on toward the land of the giants.

It was a long journey from Asgard to Jotunheim; but at last Skirnir could see through the mist the castle of Gymir, Gerd's father. It was on the top of a long, narrow mountain: a deep chasm yawned at the foot of the mountain.

Skirnir had been on so many perilous journeys and had seen so many strange sights that he knew the dangers of crossing the chasm. The heavy iron gate on the other side was shut, and the bridge was drawn up for the night, although it was not late. Skirnir could have gone no farther had it not been for his matchless steed. He spoke softly in Sleipnir's ear, and the noble creature cleared the chasm and the wall at a bound, while sharp lightning flashed, and crackling thunder sounded.

The chasm was considered such a safeguard that no watchman stood outside the castle; but two fierce dogs were chained at the entrance. As Skirnir came near, he saw a cowherd, who was resting after having sheltered his cattle for the night. He rode up to him, and said: "Tell me, cowherd, as you sit there on the mound, looking all ways, how can I pass the fierce dogs, that I may speak with Gymir's young daughter? I have a message for her."

The cowherd was struck dumb at the sight of Skirnir and at his bold words. Instead of answering his question, he stared in silence. Then he exclaimed: " You are a man doomed to die, or you are a spirit come back from the dead! No living man could have crossed the chasm and be here in this place!"

"Tell me how I may see Gymir's daughter!" interrupted Skirnir.

"Never will you speak with the good maid, Gerda," said the man.

"That I will!" cried Skirnir. "If I die in the attempt, so be it! My death is decreed for a certain day, and on that day shall I die, whether I be in Gymir's castle or elsewhere. No man can escape his fate." Just then Sleipnir becoming restless, struck the rocks with his mighty hoofs so that the very mountains trembled, and the noise of his hoofs resounded far and wide.

Gerd was in her father's hall, a serving-maid with her. When she heard the noise made by Skirnir's horse, she said to the maid: "What is that sound? The earth is shaken, and all the house of Gymir trembles!"

The maid ran to one of the rude openings and looked out. Then she turned to Gerd, saying, "A man is without; he has dismounted from his horse's back; he lets his steed browse on the grass."

"Go out," said Gerd, "and bid him come into our hall and drink of our bright mead. My parents are away, and I will show hospitality even should he be an enemy."

Skirnir left his horse and followed the serving-maid into the castle. The dogs growled, but did not offer to touch him. As he entered he saw that the vast hall and everything in it was of stone, cold and gray. At the upper end sat the giant-maiden on a high seat over which was thrown the skin of a wild beast. Her gleaming white arms and her golden hair lighted up the gloomy hall. She was very beautiful; but as Skirnir entered, she gazed at him with a cold, haughty expression. As he came near and knelt before her, she said: "Who are you, stranger? Do you belong to the race of the elves, or to the race of the gods? or are you one of the wise Vanir? Why have you come through the flaming fire to visit our halls?"

Skirnir replied: "I belong neither to the race of the elves nor to the race of the gods; nor am I one of the wise Vanir; yet I have come alone through the flaming fire to visit your halls."

"Why have you come?" demanded Gerd, imperiously.

Skirnir then told her of Frey: how he had seen her and loved her; and how he, to save Frey's life, had undertaken the dangerous journey. Skirnir's face glowed as he spoke of his friend, and told of his sunny, lovable nature, of his faithfulness in friendship, and his bravery in battle. But Gerd was untouched; she looked as cold and haughty as when Skirnir first came in.

Finding that he must use other means to win her, Skirnir drew from beneath his mantle the eleven golden apples given him by Iduna. Holding them towards the maid, he said: "Here are eleven golden apples, Gerd; these you shall have, if you will give your heart to Frey. Weariness and old age vanish at the taste of these wonderful apples."

Gerd said coldly: "Never will I accept the eleven golden apples to please any one, god or mortal. Frey and I shall never, while our lives last, live together."

Skirnir then took from his finger the precious ring made by Sindri. The stones flashed as he held it up. He told Gerd how the dwarfs made it down in the great under-world; and how, every ninth night, eight rings of equal beauty dropped from it. Any woman, even the daughter of a giant, must care for such a treasure, Skirnir thought.

Gerd was still unmoved; she said haughtily: "The ring I will not take. I have gold enough, here in Gymir's courts. I share my father's wealth."

Then Skirnir grew angry with the proud giant-maiden, who cared neither for love nor jewels. Holding high the fatal, glittering sword, he cried: "Look at this sword, young maiden! See how thin it is, how it glitters! Beneath its edge shall you fall, and your father, the old giant."

At this, Gerd rose from her seat, her blue eyes flashing with anger. "Never can you frighten the daughter of Gymir with your threats!" she cried. "Soon shall you meet my father in fight. You will learn to fear the giants then!"

Skirnir felt for a moment that he must give up—he could do no more. In his wrath he could have killed the proud girl; but that would not have helped his friend: it was her love he wanted—not her death. As Skirnir thought of Frey, dying of love, he was fired with the determination to win her for him.

Fixing his piercing eyes upon her, he said: "Listen, Gerd! What I tell you is the truth! If you, by your hard-heartedness, cause the death of Frey, beloved of all the Æsir, dearly shall you pay for your crime. You shall go far, far below Jötunheim, to Niflheim, the world of mist and darkness. All good beings will hate you; your only companions will be stony giants, who will ever stare coldly upon you with their large eyes. You will be bowed to the earth with a load of care and sorrow; terror will fill your soul; food will be loathsome to you. With bitter anguish and remorse will you think of Frey, and how you cast his love away, leaving him to die of grief. Too late will love for him fill your hard heart, and you will long for the days that might have been. All this will surely come to pass. Such are the punishments that await the enemies of the gods. Think of this, O Gerd! and then think of what may be if you will give your love to Frey and be his wife!"

In spite of his anger, Skirnir was filled with pity as he looked upon her,—so young and so fair, and so ignorant of life and love. And as he gazed, he saw her face change. The proud, cold look passed away, her bosom heaved, and she sank down, sobbing, upon the great stone seat.

When at last Gerd looked up, she was a different creature. Her expression was sweet and gentle, and her eyes beamed with the soft light of love. She gave Skirnir her hand, saying: "I never thought I should love one of that race so hated by my father; but you have conquered. If Frey should not love me now, it is I who would pine and die for him. But come!" she added; "let me give you some mead. You have had but a poor welcome to our gloomy castle."

Skirnir drank the foaming mead; and then he and Gerd planned for the meeting between herself and Frey. "I will become his wife," she said; "for I now love him as much as he loves me. The things you brought to win me, take back. I care not for them — but only for his love. Still, my parents may require some gift when they give me up to him; and whatever they ask must be given."

Skirnir agreed to this because he knew it was the only way to bring about the marriage.

He would not rest even one night in the castle, know-ing how eagerly Frey was watching for him. And while thick darkness covered the land of the giants, he sped swiftly towards the bright city of the gods.

So the fair giant-maiden became the wife of Frey; and a life of love and happiness opened before her. However, to gain the consent of her parents, Frey was forced to give them the fatal sword made by Thiassi. This was a great loss; for when the Twilight of the Gods should come, the sword would be in the hands of his enemies, to be used against him; but Frey had chosen love for his portion, and he was satisfied.

THE DEATH OF BALDUR.

Loki proposed one day that they should have some sports on the plains of Ida; and he named among other things the game of shooting at Baldur.

Toward sundown the Æsir went out upon the broad, green plain, and Baldur stood up in the midst of them. He stood there like a beautiful victim surrounded by his foes; but his face was peaceful, and he smiled to see how they enjoyed the strange sport.

At last, all had shot except Hödur. When his turn came, he had no weapon. Some say he was blind, and that was why he could not shoot. Just then Loki came up, and said, "Here is a little arrow I found the other day; perhaps this will do," and he gave Hodur a small, well-made arrow. Hödur took the arrow, fitted it to the string, and in an instant it was whizzing through the air. The next moment Baldur had fallen, pierced to the heart by the fatal weapon of mistletoe.

The gods were so astounded that at first no one moved. Then Thor sprang forward and lifted Baldur gently from the ground,— but he was dead. All eyes were now turned towards Hodur; for the Æsir did not suspect that Loki was the real author of the deed.

Still, no one sought to avenge Baldur's death; for the laws of the peace-stead, where they were, permitted no violence.

Wailing and lamenting, they took up the body and went slowly toward the palace of Gladsheim. The birds stopped singing, and the flowers drooped as the dead god passed by. When Odin saw them coming, and knew that Baldur was killed, he bowed his head, and said, "My son is dead! The light is gone from Asgard!" Frigga clasped him in her arms and vainly begged him to come back. The sorrow of Nanna, Baldur's wife, was too deep for tears. She did not speak or cry; but the color left her cheek, and her eye grew dim.

BALDUR'S FUNERAL.

BALDUR's body was placed in the great hall of his palace of "Broad-shining-splendor." He lay there as though asleep. His broad brow was peaceful, and his expression radiant and beautiful. Tall youths stood about him, clad in white and holding torches of sweet-smelling wood. Reverently they stood with bowed heads, while many came from distant places to look once more upon the purest of the gods. At intervals the youths chanted solemn hymns in a low tone; and at the end of each hymn came in the refrain, "Baldur the Beautiful is dead!"

News of his death soon reached the world of men, and great was the sorrow felt at his loss.

Men reverenced Odin for his wisdom and his might in battle; Baldur, they loved. Even the light-elves, always gay and merry, wept for Baldur; and the dwarfs, when they heard of his death, began to search for jewels to be burnt with him. The stony hearts of the giants were softened, and they came in troops to see him, bringing great trees, to be burned in the funeral pile.

Baldur's ship, Ringhorn, was the largest ship in the

world, and on that was built the funeral pile. The huge trees brought by the giants were first laid on; then smaller trees; and finally branches of all sweet-smelling woods. Over the boughs were laid mantles, beautifully wrought. Baldur's horse, richly caparisoned, was next placed upon the pile. And last, all who wished to honor the dead god brought gifts to be burnt with him. Odin gave his ring made by Sindri; Thor, a finely tempered sword; many of the goddesses brought their necklaces and bracelets; the dwarfs gave precious jewels; and the light-elves, having no possessions, strewed the pile with flowers.

When all was ready, they went to Baldur's palace. The youths who had been watching there placed the body upon a golden litter, and bore it slowly towards the ship. Behind them walked Nanna, supported by her maidens. She was clothed in white, and her long hair floated over her shoulders. The others, however, displayed all their magnificence in honor of the dead god. Odin was there with his wolves and his ravens. Frigga wore her richest garments, although her heart was sad. Frey rode the boar with the golden bristles, and Freyia was in her chariot drawn by cats. Thor had his famous goats. Many gods rode steeds of great beauty. And even Heimdall had left his post at the northern end of Bifröst, and came mounted on Goldtop, whose mane shone like the sun.

A strange procession it was; gods, giants, elves, and dwarfs, all uniting to honor the purest of the Æsir. And strange were the hymns they sang, as they slowly traversed the long road from Baldur's palace to the sea. The deep tones of the giants blended for once with the shrill, piping voices of the light-elves, as ancient battle-hymns and songs of peace rose upon the still air.

When they reached the ship, all stood silent, while Baldur's body was lifted upon the funeral pile. As the youths stepped down, they saw that Nanna had fallen, and her maidens were trying in vain to bring her back to life. Her heart had broken when she saw Baldur leaving her to go alone upon his last voyage. So they placed her beside him whom she had loved better than life itself.

Thor raised high his mighty hammer and consecrated the pile, while sharp lightnings flashed, and thunder sounded through the clear sky. The white sails were spread, the youths lighted the pile with their torches, and the ship Ringhorn left forever the shores of Asgard, and sailed towards the setting sun. As it sailed away, the smoke rose to heaven, and soon the whole ship was in flames; until at last it sank behind the western horizon in a blaze of glory.

HERMOD'S JOURNEY IN SEARCH OF BALDUR.

AFTER Baldur's death Frigga asked whether any one would be willing to go to the lower world in search of him, while preparations for his funeral were going on in Asgard. Hermod, the messenger-god, offered to go, and started off at once, on Sleipnir, the swiftest of steeds.

The Æsir watched eagerly for his return, and loud shouts went up when he appeared. He entered the great hall of Gladsheim, where all were gathered, and approaching Odin, said: "I bring you hope! Baldur greets you, and sends again this ring made by the dwarfs, which he asks you to keep always in remembrance of him." Then turning to Frigga, he gave her a carpet and other gifts from Nanna; and to Fulla, one of her maidens, a finger-ring. After bestowing these gifts, and giving each one a message from Baldur, he said:—

"I went, as you know, by the bridge Bifröst, whose northern end is near Niflheim. For nine nights Sleipnir bore me through valleys deep and dark, and at last I reached the river Gjöll, which is spanned by

the Gjaller bridge, whose roof is of glittering gold. As
Sleipnir stepped upon the bridge, the maid Modgud,
who keeps it, asked me my name and my parentage,
saying that the day before five bands of dead men
had ridden over, and had not made as much noise as
Sleipnir's hoofs made in just striking the bridge;
'And,' she added, 'it did not shake beneath them as it
does beneath you.' Then she looked closely at me, and
said: 'You have not the complexion of the dead; why do
you ride here on your way to the realms of Urd?' I told
her I came seeking Baldur, and I asked her whether he
had passed that way. She said that he had ridden over
the Gjaller bridge; and she then told me how to go,
that I might find him.

"I went as she bade me, and came at last to that
part of Mimir's realms where rules Delling, the elf of
the dawn. After going far into a thick forest I found
the castle she had described. It was as magnificent as
Gladsheim; indeed, I cannot begin to tell of its beauty
and grandeur; but it was surrounded by a wall so high
that no intruder could hope to get near. Fortunately,
I rode Sleipnir; no other steed would have served me
then. With one bound he cleared the high wall, and I
found myself in a lovely garden. Before me was the
castle. The door was open, so I stepped in; and the
first person I saw was Baldur. He sat upon a kind of
throne. Nanna was beside him. The castle was filled

with beings who were evidently rejoicing at Baldur's coming. They did not seem to be gods, and yet were fairer and nobler than mortals.

"Baldur rose to greet me as I entered, and his face beamed with the same expression of peace and good-will that it wore when he was among us. And Nanna looked as happy as on the day when she first came to Asgard as Baldur's wife. I was filled with wonder.

"Baldur said kindly : 'Hermod, you are astonished at seeing us so well and so happy here in the lower world. We have been warmly welcomed by the people who live in this beautiful castle, and their golden mead has the virtues 6f Iduna's apples, and even more; for it has restored Nanna and myself to the fullest enjoyment of life.'

"'Who are these people, Baldur?' I inquired.

"'I may not tell you all about them, Baldur replied; 'but they are my loyal subjects, and repay my love and care with the greatest devotion.'

"Then we talked of Asgard, and of you all, as we drank the golden mead. I asked Baldur whether he would return to us should the great goddess of the realms of death allow him to do so.

"He pondered deeply, and then replied, 'Yes, I would return were it allowed ; not wholly for my own pleasure — for I already love my new subjects; but because you all grieve so for my loss in the upper worlds.' And he added with a smile, 'We are very happy here.'

"When I left the palace, he and Nanna put into my hands the gifts I have brought, and seemed loath to part with me.

"From there I went south, to the land of Urd, so well known to you all. I found the mighty goddess seated by her well, her two sisters near. When I begged her to allow Baldur to return to Asgard, she said, 'Is Baldur unhappy in the lower world?'

"'No,' I replied; 'but we grieve for him in Asgard. The sun itself seems to have lost its brightness since Baldur left us; and not the gods alone, all mankind, the dwarfs and the elves, and even the stony giants, long for Baldur's return.'

"'Are you sure that *all* mourn for Baldur?' said the dread goddess, in her deep, solemn voice.

"'Yes all,' I replied.

"Then after a pause, she said slowly, 'Should every creature wish for his return, should each one weep for him, he might go back to Asgard; not otherwise. Remember, *all must weep*.'

"And so I bring you hope; for surely all will weep for Baldur; he was so loved by all."

Messengers were sent far and wide to bid all beings weep for Baldur; even the trees and stones. On swift steeds the heralds rushed along, crying, "Baldur the Beautiful is dead! Weep for him!" Over high mountains, through deep valleys, by the lonely shore, everywhere they went, crying, "Baldur the Beautiful is dead! Weep for him!" And as they heard the cry, all beings, even the rocks and the stones, wept for the god beloved of gods and men.

The messengers were going home, rejoicing in their success, when they met a giantess who called herself Thok. As she gazed at them with her cold, unfeeling eyes, they cried, "Baldur the Beautiful is dead! Weep for him!" But she answered, —

> "Thok will weep
> With dry tears
> For Baldur's death;
> Neither in life nor in death
> Gave he me gladness.
> Let Hel keep what she has."

As she spoke these words, the giantess laughed a hard, mocking laugh, and disappeared; and the messengers went slowly back to Asgard. No one knew until afterwards that the giantess was really Loki in disguise.

LOKI AT ÆGIR'S FEAST.

ÆGIR had a palace at the bottom of the ocean, in
the western part of the lower world. It was an enormous building, and its many peaks and towers seemed
to undulate as they rose through the dim waters. Near
it were forests of sea-trees that lifted their palm-like
branches as high as the castle's loftiest pinnacles. Beside the pearl walls glowed corals, red or rose-colored,
and over them ran vines of delicate green.

Ægir had asked all the gods to a feast. The huge
kettle procured by Thor and Tyr was to be used for the
first time; so there would doubtless be mead enough to
go round.

As they entered the deep-sea palace, the gods beheld
a scene of rare beauty. The large hall rose to a great
height, its roof supported by pillars of coral. From
the roof hung golden lamps, flooding the hall with
light. Sea-plants grew in all the recesses, and from
shells hidden away came sounds of low, sweet music.

The feast was spread upon a shell-shaped table. In
the centre of the table stood the giant-kettle, Mile-deep;
but so transformed that Hymir himself would not have
known it. Its pearly sides gleamed with the soft tints

of the rainbow, and around the edge was a rim of gold. It had undergone a "sea-change," and was now, indeed, "something rich and strange." Sea-youths and sea-maidens, some of them Ægir's own children, walked or rather floated about the palace; for in the deep sea no one walked as he would on the land. The maidens wore robes of green, and looked like mermaids with their long hair and their crowns of gold.

The guests were seated, and the feasting began. Ægir sat at the head of the table, with Odin beside him; while Ran, his wife, sat next Frigga.

Loki had not been invited; for, although no one could say that he had killed Baldur, all the Æsir felt that he had planned to bring about his death; and they could no longer endure his presence. But, unbidden, he appeared while they were feasting; determined to spoil their pleasure if he might not share it. He stood near the great door, looking with eyes of hate upon the fair scene. When some of the gods praised Ægir's servants, his fierce jealousy was aroused; for he could not endure to hear any one praised. And there in the presence of Ægir and the gods he slew one of the servants. Thereupon the Æsir shook their shields and drove him from the hall. He quickly disappeared in the forest of sea-trees.

They went back to their feasting; but it was not long before Loki returned. With a sneer on his lips and fierce hatred in his eyes, he asked for a drink of the mead and a seat at the table. Bragi had great cause for disliking Loki, because he had betrayed Iduna, his wife, into the hands of Thiassi; and he spoke first: "A seat and place will the Æsir never find for you at their board!" Loki answered him with taunts and sneers. Then he turned to Odin and reminded him of the oath they had sworn when both were young; and he told how, in those days, Odin refused even to taste beer unless it were offered to him also.

Not wishing to have the feast disturbed, Odin spoke to Vidar, the silent, and said, "Rise, Vidar, and let the wolf's sire sit at our feast, that he may not utter insolent words in Ægir's hall."

So Vidar rose up and presented Loki with a cup of mead; but instead of drinking, the latter began to pour out abuse upon the gods. No one escaped his venomous tongue. And, unfortunately, many of the bitter things he said were only too true; for brave and beautiful as were the gods, few of them were pure and good like Baldur. The worst he could say of Heimdall was that he had to spend his life guarding the trembling bridge.

When he reviled Frigga, she said, "False Loki, had I a son like Baldur here, you would not go out unhurt. You would be assaulted."

Then, his rage and hatred making him forget caution,

Loki replied, "Shall I tell you more of my wickedness, Frigga? I am the cause of Baldur's absence. Because of me you do not see him riding to these halls."

At these awful words the gods rose to their feet and grasped their weapons; but at a sign from Odin they restrained their wrath, and again seated themselves. No violence might be done in Ægir's halls.

Loki kept on cursing the gods until he came to Sif, Thor's wife. Thor was not there; he was far from Asgard when the Æsir were bidden to the feast. However, as Loki was abusing Sif, one of Freyia's maidens cried : "The floor of the sea trembles. I think Thor is coming from his home. He will silence this reviler of the gods !"

She was right. In a moment a noise like thunder was heard, and Thor appeared, bearing his mighty hammer. When he understood what was going on, he called out to Loki: "Silence, vile creature! My mighty hammer Miollnir shall stop your prating. I will strike your head from your neck : then your life will be ended."

Loki's fear of Thor did not prevent his uttering insulting words to him also.

Then, again, the fierce thunder-god cried in a loud voice: "Silence, vile creature! My mighty hammer Miollnir shall stop your prating. Up will I hurl you to the east region ; and no one shall ever see you again !"

Still Loki would not be silenced. In a sneering tone, he said: "Of your eastern travels you had better say little. It was there you were doubled up in a glove-thumb. You, the great hero of the gods! You hardly thought then that you were Thor."

Thor spoke again: "Silence, wretch! With this right hand, I, the terror of the giants, will smite you so that every bone shall be broken!"

Loki laughed a loud, mocking laugh, and said: "'Tis my intention to live a long life, although you do threaten me with your hammer. Skrymir's thongs seemed hard to you when you could not get at the food, —you, strong and healthy, dying of hunger!"

"Silence, monster!" cried Thor again; "my mighty hammer Miollnir shall stop your prating! I, the foe of the giants, will cast you down to hell, beneath the gratings of the dead!"

Loki spoke: "I have said before the Æsir, and I have said before the Æsir's sons, whatever my mind suggested; but for you alone will I go out, because I know that you will fight!" Then turning to Ægir, he said: "Never again shall you brew beer and hold a feast of the gods. Flames shall play over all your possessions, and you shall be burnt with them!"

With these words he darted swiftly from the hall, and they saw him no more.

THE CAPTURE OF LOKI.

Loki, after he had fled from Ægir's halls, hid among
high mountains, and there built himself a house with
four doors, which looked north, south, east, and west.
Near the house a stream rushed foaming over the rocks
into the sea. Here he lived in constant fear of the
gods; for he knew that since he had owned himself the real slayer of Baldur, they would show him
no mercy. But although he had chosen the remotest
and most secure hiding-place, Odin, from his High Seat
spied him out, and Thor and some of the other gods at
once set out to capture him.

Loki knew that the gods were coming some time
before they reached the house. And hastily casting a
fishing-net that he was making into the fire, he changed
himself into a salmon, and leaped into the neighboring
stream.

The gods entered the house, but there was no Loki.
They searched, but could not find him. As they were
looking carefully in every nook and corner, knowing
that the crafty god possessed the power of changing
himself into different shapes, one of their number
noticed something peculiar in the ashes, and called

the others to come and look. One said that it looked as though a device for catching fish had been recently thrust into the fire; and on pulling it out, they found that it was a half-burnt net. This suggested the idea that in order to elude them, Loki had changed himself into a fish, and had leaped into the stream near by.

The gods at once set to work and wove a net after the pattern of the one found in the ashes; and when it was finished, they took it to the river. Putting it in, they let it sink to the bottom. And then Thor took one end, while the other gods took the other, and thus they drew it along the stream. The wily salmon, however, thrust himself between two stones and the net passed over him. So, when the gods drew it up, they found that although it had touched some living thing, there was no fish in it.

The next time they put great weights into the net, so that it raked the bed of the river. Loki finding that he could not escape if he stayed at the bottom, and knowing that it was but a short distance to the sea, swam rapidly down the stream, and leaped over the net to where the river fell foaming over the rocks. The gods saw him as he rose above the water in his flying leap. The next time they divided themselves into two bands; and they dragged the net, while Thor followed, wading in the middle of the river. Loki must now do one of two things, — leap again over the net, up stream, or swim rapidly out to sea. He chose the former course, and leaped high into the air. But Thor was ready, and with a quick motion caught him in his hand. The salmon was so slippery that he would have escaped had not Thor had a firm grip on his tail.[1] Loki was now forced to take his proper shape; and they bound him and carried him to the lower world.

In the great judgment hall near Urd's well, his doom was pronounced. All beings who had suffered through him or who knew of his crimes were called upon to testify. Frigga charged him with the death of Baldur; Bragi, with the betrayal of Iduna; and Skadi said that he had caused the death of her father, Thiassi. All — gods, elves, dwarfs, and giants — witnessed to the harm they or their friends had suffered at the hands of the wicked god. When all the evidence was brought in, it seemed as though no punishment could be great enough for so cruel and treacherous a being.

Urd's servants took him, bound, to the dark cave near Mt. Hvergelmir. And there the iron gates were opened, and they went down to the world of darkness. Torches shed their lurid light upon the awful scenes. Here were confined many horrible monsters — giants, witches, and dragons — foes to gods and men.

After a long journey they reached the borders of a dark, sluggish sea. Taking a boat, they rowed out to a

[1] Ever since that time salmon have had very fine, thin tails.

rocky island, rising in the midst of the sea. The island was full of caves in which monsters were confined; in one was the wolf, Fenrir. They placed Loki near his offspring, binding his feet and hands with strong chains, and fastening him firmly to the rocks. The rest of his punishment was too dreadful to be told; but dreadful as it was, Loki deserved it all.

Near the rocky island was moored an enormous ship, called Nagelfar; it was larger even than Ringhorn, Baldur's ship. When Ragnarök, the Twilight of the Gods, should come, Loki would be freed from his fetters; and gathering the hosts of evil, would set sail upon this ship to fight against the gods. Then the fierce venom of his soul, nursed through long years, would flame out in deeds against his hated foes.

THE TWILIGHT OF THE GODS.

When the gods returned to Asgard, it seemed to them that everything was changed. Baldur was gone forever, and Loki, once a gay, witty companion, and later a secret and dreaded foe, was securely bound in the world of darkness. As evening fell upon the city, Odin, surrounded by the greater gods, stood looking out upon the sea, over which the ship Ringhorn had borne the dead Baldur.

All were silent, until at last Odin spoke: "Baldur has gone, and Loki is punished. A new life begins; and it is right that you, the wisest and strongest of the Æsir, should know what lies before you, and before us all. You are strong, and can bear the truth, hard though it be. You have heard that a time is coming, called the Twilight of the Gods; it is of that I will now speak." Then silence reigned again, while Odin stood with bowed head.

At last he spoke, uttering this solemn prophecy, while his eyes seemed looking into the far, dim future: "As the ages roll on, wickedness shall increase in Asgard, and in the world of men. Witches and monsters shall be bred up in the Iron-wood, and shall sow the seeds of evil in the world. Brothers shall slay each other ; cousins shall kinship violate ; shields shall be cloven ; no man will spare another. Hard shall it be in the world — an axe age, a sword age, a wind age, ere the world sinks.

"The great Fimbul winter shall come, when snow shall fall from the four corners of heaven ; deadly will be the frosts, and piercing the winds, and the darkened sun will impart no gladness. Three such winters shall come, and no summer to gladden the heart with sunshine. Then shall follow more winters, when even greater discord shall prevail. Fierce wolves shall devour the sun and moon, and the stars shall fall from heaven. The earth shall tremble, the stony hills shall be dashed together, giants shall totter, and dwarfs groan before their stony doors. Men shall seek the paths leading to the realms of death ; and earth, in flames, shall sink beneath the seething ocean.

"Then shall the aged World Tree tremble ; and loudly shall bark the dog of hell. At that sound shall the fetters of Loki and the wolf be broken ; and the Midgard serpent, with terrible lashing and struggling, shall forsake the sea. The ship, Nagelfar, shall be loosed from its moorings by the rocky isle ; and all the hosts of evil shall go on board, while Loki steers them across the sluggish sea. Surt[1] shall leave his fiery

[1] Surt was the father of Suttung, from whom Odin treacherously obtained the poetic mead — the mead that could make men poets.

dales, and join the hosts of evil, to fight against the gods.

"Loudly shall the ancient horn of Heimdall then resound throughout the nine worlds. And when they hear the sound, the hosts of Odin shall make ready; the gods and all the warriors of Valhall shall buckle on their armor for the last great fight. Odin shall seek wisdom from Mimir, that he may know how best to meet his foes.

"Terrible will be the onset when on the great plain [1] the hosts of the sons of destruction meet the armies of the gods. Then will come the second grief to Frigga, when Odin goes to meet the wolf. For then will her beloved fall. But Vidar, the great son of Odin, shall pierce the heart of Loki's offspring, and avenge his father's death. Mighty Thor will meet the Midgard serpent, and in his rage will slay the worm. Back nine paces will he go, and then fall, — he who feared no foe, — slain by the venom of the deadly beast. Tyr shall meet the fierce dog of hell, and they shall slay each other. Frey will meet his death at the hand of Surt, slain by Thiassi's fatal sword. Little shall the love of Gerd avail him on that day. Heimdall, the wise and pure, shall fall at the hand of Loki, the father of monsters, and shall in turn cause Loki's death. Few shall be left alive who meet in that great fight!"

[1] This plain was a hundred miles square.

He ceased, and there was silence, while the shadows deepened, and the sea grew dark.

Finally Tyr spoke: "And is there no hope, Odin? Does all end in darkness?" At these words Odin's face changed; a gleam of sunshine seemed to fall upon it, and he said: "I see arise, a second time, earth from ocean, beauteously green. I see waterfalls where leap the fish, and eagles flying over the hills. I see Baldur and Hodur, the rulers of a purer race of mortals, — mortals who have long served Baldur in the lower world, — and near them Vidar and the sons of Thor. They meet on Ida's plains, and call to memory the mighty deeds of the old gods, and their ancient lore. They speak of the serpent, the great earth-encircler, and of the deeds of Loki and of Thor. Unsown shall the fields bring forth, and all evil shall be done away with, when Baldur and Hodur reign."

He ceased, while his gaze seemed penetrating through the misty ages.

The silence was long; but finally one of the gods said: "And what of us, Odin? Is there no hope for the old gods?"

As he spoke, a look never before seen on his bold features overspread the face of Odin, and raising his eyes reverently, he said: "After the Twilight of the Gods, shall come the Mighty One to judgment, — He whom we dare not name, the powerful One from above, who rules over all. He shall dooms pronounce, and strifes allay, and holy peace establish, which shall be forevermore. I see a hall with gold bedecked, brighter than the sun, standing in the high heavens. There shall the righteous dwell forevermore, in peace and happiness."

As the vision faded, Odin looked upon the gods, who stood silent before him. "My children," said the All-father, "let us be strong and valiant. Long will be the ages, hard will be the fighting, and many the woes that we must endure; but the brave heart loves danger, and the strong soul shrinks not from evil and sorrow. To do our best, knowing that we shall fail; to fight to the end, and then give place to those who are wholly pure and good, — that is the fate of the old gods. He whom we may not name has so decreed it; and His decrees are ever just and right."

VOCABULARY.[1]

——◦◦◦——

IN order not to depart too far from the original pronunciation of the proper names, it may be well to observe the following rules: [2]—

a as in *far*, or shorter.

æ as the vowel sound in *there*.

e as e in *let*.

i as ee in *need*, or shorter.

ei, both vowels sounded.

o as in *rode*.

ö should have a sound resembling the vowel sound in *heard*; it has no English equivalent.

u as oo in *mood*, or shorter.

y as u in French; there is no English equivalent.

j as y in *young*.

s always sharp.

th in *Thor* and some other words has the sound of th in *father*.

v as w in *well*.

Ægir, god of the stormy sea.   In provincial English they still say, "Have a care! there is the *eager* coming."

Æsir or **Asas**, the gods ruled over by Odin.

Alfheim (elf-land), given to Frey as a tooth-gift.

Allfather, one of Odin's many names.

Asgard, the home of the Æsir.

---

[1] In the spelling of the proper names Thorpe has been followed, in most cases, rather than Anderson, as Thorpe gives the final *i* and *ir* instead of *e* and *er*. In the definitions Anderson has been followed. All accents except the umlaut have been omitted.

[2] The rules for pronunciation are based upon the rules in Sweet's Icelandic Primer, a book that deals with Old Icelandic in its classical period, between 1200 and 1350.

Ask (ash), the name of the first man created by Odin, Hœnir, and Lodur.

Asynjur, the goddesses.

Audhumbla, the cow formed from the frozen vapor.

Baldur (the best; the foremost), the god of the summer sunlight.

Bestla came from under Ymir's arm; Mimir's sister; Odin's mother.

Bifröst (to tremble), the bridge of the gods. The Milky Way or the rainbow.

Bilskirnir (a-moment-shining), Thor's palace.

Bor, son of Bur.

Bur or **Bure,** father of Bor, progenitor of the Æsir and Vanir; produced by the cow's licking the rime-stones.

Breidablik (broad-blink; broad-shining), Baldur's dwelling.

Brisingamen, Freyia's necklace, made by the dwarfs.

Brok, a dwarf; Sindri's brother.

Draupnir (to drip), Odin's ring, made by the dwarfs.

Delling (dayspring), the elf of the dawn; the father of day.

Egil, guardian of the spring Hvergelmir; one of the race of Ivaldi.

Embla, the first woman, formed from a tree.

Fenrir, the monster-wolf, son of Loki. He kills Odin, and is killed by Vidar, at Ragnarök.

Fimbul-winter, the great and awful winter preceding the destruction of the world.

Forsete, the peace-maker, son of Baldur and Nanna.

Frey, son of Niörd; a Van; ruler over the light-elves.

Freyia, sister of Frey and daughter of Niörd. Half the fallen in battle belong to her.

Frigg or **Frigga** (love), wife of Odin and queen of the gods.

Fulla, one of Frigg's maidens.

Gerd, daughter of the giant Gymir, beloved by Frey.

Giallar-bridge, the bridge between the living and the dead, in the under-world.

Giallar-horn, Heimdall's horn, which he will blow at Ragnarök.

Gimli or **Gimill** (heaven), the abode of the righteous after Ragnarök.

Ginungagap, the chaos or formless void before creation. In the eleventh century the sea between Greenland and Vinland (America) was called Ginnunga-gap.

Gladsheim (home of brightness or gladness), Odin's palace.

Gleipnir, the last fetter with which the wolf Fenrir was bound.

Goldtop, Heimdall's horse.

Gymir, a giant, the father of Gerd.

Heimdall, the son of nine mothers; guardian of the northern end of Bifröst.

Hel (according to Rydberg), a general name for all the under-world, and a special name for the regions south of Hvergelmir.

Hermod, son of Odin.

Hödur, the slayer of Baldur.

Hrimfaxi (rime-mane), the horse of night.

Hœnir (according to Rydberg), the same as Vili, Odin's brother.

Hugi, the one who raced with Thialfi; Utgard-Loki's "thought."

Hugin (mind), one of Odin's ravens. His two ravens flew over the nine worlds each day.

Hvergelmir (the old kettle), the spring in the middle of Niflheim, the lower giant-world; from it flowed twelve rivers.

Hymir, a giant, owner of the kettle Mile-deep.

Ida's Plains, in Asgard.

Idunn or **Iduna**, daughter of Ivaldi, goddess of early spring; possessor of the golden apples.

Ivaldi, father of Thiassi and other artists; also father of Idunn.

Jötunheim, home of the giants. There were two regions inhabited by giants, one on the same plane with Midgard (but the other side of the river Ocean), and the other in the great under-world. The latter was called Niflheim.

Leding, one of the fetters with which the wolf Fenrir was bound.

Lif, **Lifthrasir**, mortals, called Asmegir, preserved by Mimir in the under-world; ruled over by Baldur after his death. Their descendants were to re-people the earth after Ragnarok.

Lodur (according to Rydberg), identical with Vei, a brother of Odin; one of the gods who created Ask and Embla.

Logi (wild-fire), the one who contended with Loki in eating.

Loki (to end; to finish), the evil giant-god of Norse mythology.

Manheim, the same as Midgard.

Midgard (the mid-yard or middle-town), the abode of men, surrounded by the river Ocean.

Midgard-serpent, Loki's offspring; he was put into the river Ocean.

Mimir, the wisest being in the nine worlds; he grew from under the arm of Ymir; guarded the well of wisdom. Rydberg calls him "the most characteristic figure" of northern mythology.

Munin (memory), one of Odin's ravens.

Miöllnir or **Mjölnir,** Thor's hammer.

Modgud, the maid who kept the Giallar-bridge.

Muspelheim, the fiery world.

Nagelfar, the ship in which Loki sails with the "sons of destruction," to fight against the gods.

Nanna, daughter of Nep (bud), wife of Baldur.

Niflheim (mist; fog), home of the giants in the under-world.

Niörd, a Van-god, husband of Skadi, and father of Frey and Freyia. He dwelt in Noatun, in the western part of the under-world.

Noatun, Niörd's home.

Norns, the weird sisters; the three heavenly norns, Urd, Verdande, and Skuld (Past, Present, and Future). They guarded the sacred well under Yggdrasil's third root, and decided what should be the life of each human being.

Odin or **Wodan,** son of Bor and Bestla, the ruler of the Æsir. He is the fountain-head of wisdom, the founder of culture, the lord of battle and victory. Wednesday is named for him.

Ragnarök, the last day; the Twilight of the Gods.

Ran, wife of the sea-god Ægir. She caught drowning men in her net, and took them to her palace.

Raska or **Röskva,** the peasant-girl who went with Thor to Utgard-Loki's.

Ratatösk, a squirrel that ran up and down the branches of Yggdrasil.

Rune, one of the characters forming the earliest alphabet of the Teutonic nations. Runes had magic properties.

Sif, Thor's wife.

Sindri, a dwarf, one of the " original artists "; a maker of wonderful things.

Skadi, a giantess; daughter of Thiassi and wife of Niörd.

Skidbladnir, Frey's ship, made by the sons of Ivaldi.

Skinfaxi (shining-mane), the horse of day.

Skirnir (identical with Svidpag and with Hermod, Rydberg maintains), Frey's friend.

Skrymir, the giant (Utgard-Loki in disguise) who met Thor in the forest.

Sleipnir, Odin's eight-legged horse, the swiftest of steeds.

Surt, the representative of subterranean fire. The father of Suttung, from whom Odin treacherously stole the poetic mead. He joins the "sons of destruction" at Ragnarök.

Thialfi, son of a peasant who goes with Thor to Utgard-Loki's.

Thiassi, a giant and an artist; son of Ivaldi.

Thok, Loki disguised as a giantess.

Thor, the thunder-god; the foe of the giants.

Thrym, a giant who stole Thor's hammer.

Twilight of the Gods, the last day; Ragnarök.

Tyr, the one-armed god of war. Tuesday is named for him.

Urd, the chief of the three norns; queen of the dead.

Urda fount, Urd's fountain.

Utgard (the out-yard), the abode of Utgard-Loki.

Utgard-Loki, the giant king who lives in Utgard.

Valfather (father of the slain), one of Odin's names.

Valhall or **Valhalla** (the hall of the slain), the hall to which Odin invited those slain in battle.

Valkyrie or **Valkyrja** (the chooser of the slain). The Valkyries were a troop of goddesses, handmaidens of Odin. They served in Valhall, and were sent on Odin's errands.

Vanir or **Vans,** gods, akin to the Æsir; their home was in the under-world, but some of them lived in Asgard.

Vanaheim, the abode of the Vanir.

Vor or **Var,** the goddess of betrothals and marriages.

Ve or **Vei,** and **Vili,** Odin's brothers; with their help he formed the world.

Vegtam, an assumed name of Odin's.

Vidofnir, a cock that glitters on the topmost bough of Yggdrasil.

Yggdrasil (the bearer of Ygg [Odin]), the world-embracing ash-tree.

Ymir, the first living being. Out of his body Odin and his brothers formed the world.

REFERENCES.

Introductory Chapter. { The Vala's Prophecy. The Lay of Vafthrûdnir. The Lay of Grimnir. } Sæmund's Edda.
The Fooling of Gylfe. The Younger Edda.
Anderson's Norse Mythology. } Account of the Creation.

Odin seeks Wisdom from Mimir. { The lines quoted from Odin's Rune-Song, Sæmund's Edda.
Chapters on Mimir in Rydberg's Teut. Myth. begin p. 208.

The Binding of the Wolf. } The Fooling of Gylfe. The Younger Edda.

Baldur the Beautiful. { From scattered passages in both Eddas. Rydberg's Teut. Myth., p. 304.

Baldur's Dreams. { The Lay of Vegtam.   Sæmund's Edda. The Fooling of Gylfe.   The Younger Edda. Rydberg's Teut. Myth., pp. 240 and 248–9.

Loki makes trouble between the Artists and the Gods. { The Lay of Grimnir (a slight allusion). Sæmund's Edda. The Poetical Diction. The Younger Edda. Rydberg's Teut. Myth., pp. 115 and 593.

How Thiassi captured Loki. The Gods grow old. Loki brings back Iduna. } Bragi's Talk. The Younger Edda. Rydberg's Teut. Myth., pp. 650–656.

Thor and Skrymir. { Ægir's Compotation, or Loki's Altercation. Sæmund's Edda. The Fooling of Gylfe.   The Younger Edda.

Thor's Journey to get the Kettle for Ægir.	The Lay of Hymir. Sæmund's Edda. The Fooling of Gylfe. The Younger Edda. Anderson's Norse Mythology. A translation of Œlenschlæger's poem, " Thor's Fishing," by Longfellow.
Thor and Thrym.	The Lay of Thrym. Sæmund's Edda.
Frey climbs into Odin's High Seat.	The Journey or Lay of Skirnir. Sæmund's Edda.
Skirnir's Journey to win Gerd for Frey.	The Fooling of Gylfe. The Younger Edda.
The Death of Baldur. Hermod's Journey in search of Baldur.	The Vala's Prophecy. } Sæmund's Edda Ægir's Compotation. } (allusions). The Fooling of Gylfe. The Younger Edda. Rydberg's Teut. Myth., pp. 248–256.
Loki's Abuse of the Gods at Ægir's Feast.	Ægir's Compotation, or Loki's Altercation. Sæmund's Edda. The Poetical Diction. The Younger Edda.
The Capture of Loki.	The Lay of Vegtam. Sæmund's Edda (an allusion). The Fooling of Gylfe. The Younger Edda. Rydberg's Teut. Myth., p. 189.
The Twilight of the Gods.	The Vala's Prophecy. Sæmund's Edda. The Fooling of Gylfe. The Younger Edda. Rydberg's Teut. Myth., pp. 376–385.